CE

During the last ten years, governments have taken an increasingly active interest in industry. The reasons for this have not been entirely understood either by the general public or, even, by management and the trade unions. Politicians have done little to explain the change and, as a result, many people, including Enoch Powell, see government involvement as part of a definite philosophy or "socialist conspiracy".

Nothing could be further from the truth. Indeed, if there had ever been a systematic approach to government intervention in industry—to sponsorship, R. & D. support, industrial relations, and the rest—let alone a philosophy, many of the difficulties and failures in decision-making which exist today could have been avoided.

Eric Moonman was, until recently, chairman of the Parliamentary Labour Party's Science and Technology Committee, and is admirably equipped to write this book. His frank and courageous analysis of what has gone wrong spares neither of the Parliamentary front benches. But his book does more than provide a critique of the relationship between government and industry: it offers a number of practical and well-developed proposals for making both government and industry more effective.

RELUCTANT PARTNERSHIP

ERIC MOONMAN was Member of Parliament for Billericay, 1966-70. Born in 1929 in Liverpool, he left school at the age of thirteen. He attended night school classes before going to university. He is married with two children.

He became chairman of the Parliamentary Labour Party's Science and Technology Committee; a member of the House of Commons Select Committee (Science and Technology); a governor of Imperial College of Science and Technology; and formerly Parliamentary Private Secretary to the Secretary of State for Education and Science. Until 1966 he was Senior Research Fellow at the University of Manchester Institute of Science and Technology.

His publications include *The Manager and the Organization* (Tavistock and Pan); *Science and Technology in Europe* (Penguin); *Communication in an Expanding Organisation* (Tavistock); and numerous articles in the press and business journals both in Britain and in America.

RELUCTANT PARTNERSHIP

A CRITICAL STUDY OF
THE RELATIONSHIP BETWEEN
GOVERNMENT AND INDUSTRY

ERIC MOONMAN, M.Sc.

LONDON
VICTOR GOLLANCZ LTD
1971

*To the fond memory
of my parents*

MADE AND PRINTED IN GREAT BRITAIN BY
THE GARDEN CITY PRESS LIMITED
LETCHWORTH, HERTFORDSHIRE

CONTENTS

AUTHOR'S NOTE

I wish to record my grateful thanks to the various friends and colleagues who have helped in the preparation of this book: Mrs. C. Hawks, Mr. P. Routledge and, in particular, Audrey Cozens and my wife, Jane.

AN APPRAISAL OF CURRENT
GOVERNMENT/INDUSTRIAL
RELATIONS

Evidence of stresses in the relations between government and industry is presented to us almost daily. The medium- and long-term strategy involved in recent government policies has angered not only industry but also the City and the business world, while on the shop floor the apparent need for improvement in wages and conditions of service has brought the unions into conflict with the government's economic plans. The resulting Industrial Relations White Paper containing penal clauses provoked a predictably hostile reaction from the trade unions and the Labour movement in general—so much so that the offensive clauses were eventually dropped, causing in turn an outcry from the Confederation of British Industry.

What are the underlying reasons for contemporary industrial criticism of government? The first and most likely cause is the inevitable reaction by industry to a government which has urged efficiency yet has apparently neglected to put its own house in order. In the last decade shoddy work-practices and inefficiency have been exposed at every level of industry by the appropriate government departments and related bodies like the British Productivity Council. Whilst individual employers may privately admit the justification for such action and the need for improvement, they are not prepared to welcome it from an organ of government that can be equally inefficient.

A second cause may be found in the very concept of State economic and industrial planning, associated as it is with a number of emotive terms such as nationalization, exchange control and taxation. Governments, Labour Governments in particular, have become more involved in the running of industry. Yet public reaction to government intervention is not always negative. From time to time the return, usually overwhelmingly, of a Labour government, constitutes demand for more state interference in order to ensure a better overall service in, for instance, the social services, education and welfare facilities.

A third reason can be found in the ambivalence—at times even failure—of some of the government's industrial policies. Its assessment of how to bring about improvements has frequently been naïve. It is not enough to set up the machinery whereby industry can talk to government. In the early 1960s, economic growth was acknowledged to be the essential forerunner of improvements in housing, education and private consumption. The term "growth" became a key political slogan and the public came to expect a rapid and continuous improvement in living standards. But economic growth cannot be achieved by politicians; it depends on factors far beyond their control and on men outside their influence : on investors, on exporters, on financiers. It became obvious that in order to make economic growth a reality, government had to influence industrial and commercial policy decisions.

As a result of such causes as these, combined with the Labour Party's indifferent image and the general uncertainty of government involvement in industry, a large section of the business community now reacts hysterically even to the mere mention of government action. Certainly, mistakes have been made, but such automatic hostility is hardly fair in view of the many practical facilities which the government can provide and has. Often, too, the government gets the blame for a company's own failure to assess accurately its industrial or structural problems. A smaller firm is particularly prone to this type of error and proportionately is more susceptible to the harsh effect of the application of a government squeeze, very often made still worse by its own structural limitations.

The smaller business will argue that governments simply do not understand their difficulties, claiming that this is inevitable because of the contrast in the organization structure of the two, government being highly formalized and rigid, and the small firm being essentially flexible. The small firm relies on its flexibility to meet uncertainty in trading conditions—recruiting workers more freely and making adjustments more rapidly than the larger unit. A common weakness in the smaller firm is lack of capital, and failure to secure an increase in overdraft facilities or trade credit from suppliers can mean financial stress, and even liquidation. Government policies introduced in the autumn of 1966—a combination of SET, a squeeze on bank loans and a check on sales of consumer goods—made conditions for small firms difficult; and added to this our current business trends are apt to prove intolerant of the small unit. For example, so far as the management aspect is concerned, the traditional capitalism of a hundred years ago meant that a large number of small, independent and specialized firms were run by businessmen who generally had experience of all aspects of the business and maintained effective control over them. They knew the problems they had to deal with and they could see to it that their decisions were carried out without being distorted or frustrated in the process. If the decisions were sound the rewards were substantial; but, similarly, if they failed the penalties were severe. The close identity between ownership and management had a direct effect on decision-making. Today, except in really small firms, this close identity has largely disappeared. Management specialists, shared decision-making, national wage agreements, national and local association procedures: such things now influence managerial decisions to such a degree that even small firms have tended to become much less integrated than they were.

A detailed review of the Labour government's record would show that there were errors in the implementation of industrial policies which naturally widened the rift between the government and industry. We saw, more than once, that the already precarious relations between the two were aggravated in the years 1964–70. Labour began in 1964 with a great deal of goodwill from the public and from many in the business world and the City. The Labour government inherited several enormously serious problems which, it was argued several years after, required much tougher measures than they were prepared to introduce at that time. On the balance of payments, they inherited in the final quarter of 1964 a deficit on current account that was running at an annual rate of just over £400 million, and a deficit on long-term capital account that was running at an annual rate of just under £400 million. A year later, in November 1965, some improvements had been made, yet Labour's policy was to rely on temporary restraints in imports. Industry also argued for more incentives of a permanent kind to stimulate exports but there was little forthcoming from the government. Yet, in reducing the long-term capital deficit, Labour's achievements were considerable. One reliable economic commentator was forced to admit, at this time, "that foreign confidence in Labour's government is growing. Anybody who talked to foreign central bankers in recent weeks must report that they now regard Mr. Wilson as a most thoroughly respectable chap." This was just about the same view the British people including the industrialists had of the Prime Minister at the time. British businessmen were still attracted by the fact that here was a technocrat government which, even if they did not understand or like its socialist label, might at least be an improvement over the previous stop-go-stop cycles which made company forecasting so tough. The socialists thought well of themselves, too. Norman MacKenzie, writing a piece in line with *New Statesman* philosophy of the time (14 May 1965), said that "the transfer from the opposition benches for Labour had brought about a massive change in decision making".

Ministers now have access to a huge civil service machine capable of feeding them with facts and ideas on a scale unthinkable for Transport House. They can appoint committees and commissions at will. Academics trip over themselves to become consultants, or even to be asked for their opinions, whilst a host of public and private organizations provide information or advice to the government that no party official could hope to obtain from them. The difference this makes to those translated from opposition to office is little short of miraculous.

Andrew Shonfield in the *Listener* (3 March 1966), "Labour Britain", euphorically described relations between business and government as so good that the salaries of big businessmen, loaned for a couple of years at a time to the Labour government, would continue to be paid by their companies whilst they worked in Whitehall. He declared, "there could hardly be a more dramatic celebration of the burying of the class war". It sounded fine; unfortunately someone forgot to tell the trade union movement.

When in March 1966 the British public endorsed the Wilson administration with a strong majority, instead of the precarious handful of eighteen months previously, it seemed that all sections of society including industry would present a united front for solving the country's economic problems. What went wrong? My own interpretation of the situation is that the Labour government adopted and modified a basically Conservative policy and took the acquiescence of its traditional supporters in these plans too much for granted. To many of the rank and file it seemed that the government's economic policies relied too much on the responses of the suppliers of capital and too little on organized labour. The Prices and Incomes legislation saw the departure in large numbers of the government's natural allies. The removal of this safety net left Labour in an exposed position when the employers too—both individually and through the CBI—became disenchanted. The growth-knockers were now out in force. At the beginning of 1967, problems of structure and decision-making were beginning to emerge: the point and purpose of economic policies was being questioned openly by civil servants as well as by politicians. It is probably a harsh judgement, but to many in industry, Ministers appeared to dabble in policies and then apparently forget them. The disappearance of the National Plan, with its targets and proposals to help industry, was further evidence to some that Labour did not know the first thing about industrial decision-making.

So industry disliked the way government acted. Ironically, their dislike could not be attributed to the *implementation* of the Prices and Incomes Policy. On the contrary, it was the failure of the government's control of the price increase mechanism which brought about public indignation. Wages and salaries were held back but there was not the same thoroughness in controlling prices. The DEP tried hard to make some semblance of success out of a difficult situation. Indeed by late 1968 it was fair to say that the battle for productivity had largely been won. The DEP had, without doubt, played an important role in involving a large number of people in productivity talks and bargains. The government's prices control policy was more difficult to implement. Unlike productivity or wages, prices are not an easily identifiable area of responsibility to allocate within the government structure, although DEP took the lion's share. The PIB has been a valuable tool in providing information and undertaking research but it is in the area of action that criticism remains.

One of the extraordinary features of the debate which continued throughout this period of Labour government, on the macro- and micro-levels of the economy, was the way in which the Prime Minister was held so personally responsible for all that had happened. Once the debate was brought to such personal terms, the intellectual arguments were fudged and even passed over. When the Conservative press mounted its more virulent articles on Mr. Wilson, it merely helped to establish his authority within the Parliamentary Labour Party. In consequence, discussion of economic and industrial progress was relegated to the background to its great disadvantage.

By September 1968, a special mid-term manifesto was produced in which Labour promised to do better. The hard measures begun in the budget a few months before were endorsed. It was an honest statement full of good intentions but there was no integrated account of Labour's future economic policy.

The CBI made much noise about Labour's inability to understand industrial affairs. In a balance sheet which they prepared for propaganda purposes to protest against government cuts in business entertainment expenses and against the Corporation Tax and Selective Employment Tax, they actually showed how substantial cuts in public expenditure had released money for other essential services!

The cuts included: TSR2 military aircraft cancellation—6 April 1965; Local Authority mortgages cut from £180m to £130m; other public projects slowed—27 July 1965; Public Spending cut by £100m, defence spending cut by £100m—20 July 1966; Defence spending cut by £75m with a future ceiling of £2,000 a year—18 July 1967; Public Spending cut £100m, defence spending cut £100m—18 Nov. 1967; Public spending to be cut by £300m in 1968/69 and £416m in 1969/70; the package included withdrawal East of Aden, postponement of the rise in the school leaving age, end of free school milk for secondary schools, increased health charges and cuts in housing, roads and research—16 Jan. 1968.

There are, of course, two sides to this kind of argument, but, when it came to the point, the Tory party proved singularly unable to exploit Labour's distress. Too often its front bench in the House chose the wrong subject for attack whilst back-benchers laboured points which, to the electorate, must have seemed irrelevant.

As a result industry showed signs of losing patience with its parliamentary spokesmen on the Tory side. Attacks came from outside the House. Eric Caswell, a member of the CBI council and chairman of the Metal Window Association, read a paper in which he launched a violent attack on the Labour government and drew unfavourable parallels with the previous Conservative administration. The paper asked pointedly how long industrialists could continue to co-operate with the Labour government, and in the discussion which followed, there was much support for an open campaign by British industrialists to rid the country of its infamous government.

Leaving on one side the huff and the puff of the politicians, the CBI, and the trade unions, there have, even so, been

examples when despite good, sincere government intentions of
aiding industry, the idea or scheme has backfired. The Industrial
Liaison Officers scheme is a case in point. Few would deny that
the concept of having a better linking system between colleges,
universities, local firms and the Ministry of Technology was
worthy of support. In practice, however, the never easy task of
the ILOs was made more difficult by the curious measure-of-
performance scheme devised by the Ministry. Every six months
a list was drawn up to rate the eighty officers. The main
criterion in the rating was the number of visits made to industry.
Other criticisms of the service are that a large number of write-
ups are required, although there is little evidence that the case
papers are ever acted upon; there is also a good deal of duplication of effort with other management technique visitors, for
example, the IRO, Training Board Staff, the BPC and BIM.
Another major failure of Government good intentions, the
nuclear power industry, is dealt with in detail in a later chapter.

So much for the Labour government's relations with industry.
Unsatisfactory as they were, it is at least arguable that things
would have been much the same whichever political party was in
power. There is a certain inevitability about the present strain
in the relations between government and industry. While it may
be true that the Labour Party is more consciously dedicated to
the planning and direction of industrial affairs, and to that
extent rouses more vocal opposition, the size and scope of
modern industry is such that no government can afford a policy
of *laissez-faire*. The social consequences cannot be left to private
enterprise to deal with. If total state control is rejected as the
preferred method for controlling the activities of industry in
accordance with the needs of the nation as seen by the government of the day, we are left, "for better, for worse, for richer,
for poorer", with a reluctant partnership. It is this partnership,
how it came about, and what its future is, that is the subject of
this book.

In examining this relationship, it is necessary to look at the
influences, the errors and inhibiting forces as well as at the way
in which the quality of decision-making may be improved. One

thing is abundantly clear : frequent reference to the idea of a partnership between government and industry by government is no substitute for a well-thought-out assessment by all parties of their respective roles within such a partnership. The idea must be more than a catch-phrase. The large number of government committees, panels and advisory bodies may have a valid role within the relationship, but they cannot take the place of a clearly defined policy on industrial affairs. As Professor Ben Roberts has said, speaking of collective bargaining :

"Events are compelling change in our industrial relations system. Care must be taken not to destroy that which is sound and good, but there is greater danger in refusing to recognize the need to reshape our institutions and to alter their traditional functions. Most important of all is the need to work out a new balance of relations between government, employers and unions that will facilitate the process of technological, economic and social change in the interest of all sections of the community."[1]

That balance requires examination at all levels, beginning with the protagonists themselves.

[1] B. C. Roberts (ed.), *Industrial Relations: Contemporary Problems and Perspective*, Methuen & Co., Ltd., Revised edn. 1968.

2

THE STRUCTURE AND DEVELOPMENT OF BRITISH INDUSTRY

An ANALYSIS OF industry is central to this study. When the nature of government is examined it will be seen that it was the development of industry during the nineteenth century and the social change it brought in its wake which largely shaped the development of government in this period. It is only since the end of the Second World War that the idea of government shaping industry has taken root.

What, then, is meant by "industry"? Any definition must be subject to qualifications taking into account individual differences in scale, development and geographical distribution. Some generalizations may, however, be made about the total industrial setting. These will be set out as we proceed to show the characteristics shared by all industrial units. Industry may be seen as an organism subject to constant modification. The degree of pressure will depend not only on the factors above but also on managerial and organizational systems, whether in a science-based or a traditional process unit. The term "industry" must also include all those who work for it, share responsibility for it, or support it in economic, financial, or simple human terms.

A contemporary view must also take into account the changes in industry since Marx formulated his theory more than a century ago. The intervening years have seen industrialization take a variety of economic and political forms. There is infinitely more data on which to formulate a general view of the industrial process. The *Oxford English Dictionary* says that the prevalent senses of the word "industry" are "systematic work or labour; habitual employment in some useful work . . . especially in the productive arts or manufacture; a particular form or branch of productive labour; a trade or manufacture". As a tentative, working definition, incorporating all the above elements, the following is offered: A series of organizations each having its own structure, internal mechanisms and dynamic, and consisting of men and women serving in various capacities to manufacture or produce a product or to provide a service, and, in so doing, achieving a profit on the capital employed.

To devise ways and means of analysing the processes of communication between government and industry, it is necessary to trace the historical development of business in its environment, and to identify the main areas of transition which determine the pattern of change. Two aspects of the subject which require particular attention are—the shift over the last century in the ownership and control of business, and the rapid and extensive growth in size and scale which has occurred for several reasons, foremost of these being technological and scientific advance and the influence of the American companies. Before considering these particular changes, however, it would be advisable to consider industrial development within the larger context of national growth and development.

British Industry Before 1914

The outbreak of the First World War brought to an end a century of expansion in British industrial output. During the nineteenth century, both population and living standards improved fourfold and the economic structure of the country changed profoundly. During the period 1815–75, the rate of industrial expansion averaged 3–4 per cent per annum, double that of the eighteenth century. At the same time, however, at the end of the Napoleonic Wars, 34 per cent of the employed population was still engaged in agriculture and fishing.[1] The new machine era had begun, but the full effects of this were yet to be experienced—generally the industrial framework was unstable, undeveloped and highly specialized. For instance, the

[1] J. H. Dunning and C. J. Thomas, *British Industry: Change and Development in the Twentieth Century,* Hutchinson, 1961.

application of steam power and new mechanical devices was retarded by a lack of skilled engineers, both to produce and to operate the machinery; industrial chemistry was in its early stages; there were no railways and few good roads; and the transformation of the banking system and the capital market had not been accomplished. During the first three-quarters of the century, however, England became the most highly industrialized country in the world. This rate of industrial growth was accelerated by a technology which was particularly favourable to the British economic environment. In the nineteenth century, the output of manufacturing industry increased fourteenfold whilst the proportion of the working population employed in agriculture and fishing fell to 8 per cent.[1] The relative importance of transport, commerce and the distribution industries increased as agriculture declined, and by 1914 England was dependent on manufacturing exports to finance three-quarters of her consumption of raw materials (excluding coal) and one-half of her food. One of the unique characteristics of this period of rapid growth and change was that conditions allowed Britain to consolidate her initial lead and take the fullest advantage of technological innovations, improvements in transport and communications and the liberalization of trade, without the restrictions of foreign competition.

After 1880 the rate of industrial growth fell to less than 2 per cent per annum whilst Germany's rose to 3.9 per cent and that of the US to 4.8 per cent. This was largely because Germany and the United States emerged as competitive powers to challenge Britain's early monopoly and because the development of new technology was less suited to the UK's resources. After 1900, for example, Britain was replaced by the United States as the largest supplier of coal and by Germany as the chief producer of industrial chemicals. It was the scientific prowess of Germany and the large-scale production methods of the United States which endangered British industry during the last quarter of the nineteenth century. Nevertheless, during this period of decline, or rather perhaps instability, the rate of expansion of

[1] *Ibid.*

industrial production, output per head and real wages continued to advance and new industries such as bulk steel, electrical and bicycle manufacture came into being.

Between 1820 and 1914, the producer-goods industries had a substantially higher rate of growth of output than the consumer-goods industries. Hoffman points out a corresponding relationship between the decline of industrial output at the end of the nineteenth century and non-industrial sectors of the economy, such as shipping and railways, and perhaps more interestingly, population.[1] Both population and industrial output rose rapidly in the eighteenth century, reaching the highest level of expansion in 1800. There was a close relationship between the two rates of growth throughout the nineteenth century, both declining at the end of the century. Generally speaking, however, industrial growth was the cause of rather than the result of social change.

The industrial structure of the nineteenth century brought with it changes in the geographical distribution of economic activities, though these changes were due to "natural" causes rather than deliberate planning. There was a tendency for geographic areas to concentrate on those activities in which their comparative advantages were greatest. Thus Durham, for example, let its minor trades slip away in favour of the higher rates of profit which could be earned in iron manufacture and shipbuilding.[2] Some areas increased in economic importance as a result of redistribution of industries; because they were able to seize the opportunities offered for new types of enterprise. Other areas, which had a large proportion of stagnating or decaying industries had difficulty in transferring their resources to new types of production, and these grew comparatively little in industrial content. Lancashire was the major case in point. The total employed population of that county increased very little between 1911 and 1951, by 8 per cent compared with nearly

[1] W. Hoffman, *British Industry, 1700-1950*, Basil Blackwell, Oxford, 1955.
[2] H. A. Mess, *Industrial Tyneside*.

25 per cent in Britain as a whole.[1] This comparative stagnation can be attributed to the misfortunes of Lancashire's chief industries, especially the cotton industry.

Generally speaking, whenever great changes in techniques or organization occur, the chief centres of an industry will have difficulty in maintaining their position if they cling to the processes and methods which have brought success in the past. It is also true to say that in the nineteenth century no real attention was paid to the consequence of the locational patterns of industry from the viewpoint of the economic well-being of either a particular region or of the country as a whole. The *laissez-faire* philosophy considered in connection with the history of government and the expanding economy precluded the necessity for an industrial location policy.

There was a corresponding change in the structure of industry during the nineteenth century, though significantly this was not as great as the economic or geographic development. Sometimes the increase in the size of an industry which accompanied the change in its functions, took place without any major modification of its structure. More usually, however, a new type of industrial organization was required and the merchant was replaced by the manufacturer with his factory operated by power machinery. Production for a wide market was assisted by new forms of transport involving increases in the mechanical equipment of society and thereby creating a need for new large-scale industries. Viewed more widely, however, British industrial structure continued to be dominated by a multiplicity of small, independent and individualistic business units until the First World War. Even until the late 1870s, as Dunning points out, there was an almost complete absence of an important monopolistic arrangement in British industry. And there was no attempt by the State to intervene in the course of economic affairs. In some ways, however, there was a definite movement towards larger production units and the concentration of output. The rise of the limited joint stock company and the improve-

[1] G. C. Allen, *British Industries and Their Organization*, Longmans, 4th ed., 1959.

ment of loan facilities at the turn of the century facilitated expansion of established concerns. Collective agreements made before 1914 were mainly between firms making similar products. One reason for amalgamation was the destructive competition from overseas. Thus, the threat of competition from the American Tobacco Company in Britain was met by the merger of thirteen UK tobacco manufacturers in 1901 to form the Imperial Tobacco Company.

British Industry Since 1914

In 1914, though still a major industrial power, the United Kingdom was structurally maladjusted in relation to the world economic trends then emerging. Though many important innovations of the late nineteenth century originated in Britain, economic and social conditions often favoured their more speedy commercial exploitation elsewhere. For example, early developments in motor engineering and the internal combustion engine occurred in the United Kingdom and Europe, but because of ideal circumstances in American industry, the United States was the first country to move from the experimental stage into large-scale production in the motor industry. This was partially due to centralized administration and concentrated production which were restricted in England because of *laissez-faire* principles. Furthermore, in contrast to the US, where the economy was designed to meet the needs of the new technology and where innovations were highly regarded, UK businessmen were often held back by restrictive legislation, particularly in the electrical and motor-car industries, and the expensive patent procedure often completely paralysed the exploitation of new inventions and techniques.

For eighteen months after the First World War there was a boom period which was followed by a decade of chronic depression and unemployment. One difficulty was the failure of the United Kingdom to grasp the opportunities offered by world trade in new industrial commodities. The economic atmosphere of the 1920s was not particularly favourable to the expansion of new industries or to the innovations of British

scientists. For example, the carbon-tetrachloride fire-extinguisher
and the transfer machinery of motor cars were exploited by
other countries. Both the War and its aftermath provided a
considerable impetus to development, not only in such specialized spheres as wireless and telecommunications, new stainless
steels and synthetic chemicals, and ship propulsion, but generally in stimulating organized co-operative research and the
growing intervention of the State in industrial affairs. An
important example of State "aid" was the introduction of the
McKenna import duties in 1915 which helped significantly to
support development in the motor industry. The McKenna
duties were initially imposed as a war-time measure to maintain
the foreign exchanges and to discourage expenditure on luxury
items, but remained in effect until 1932.

Following internal industrial difficulties in the 1920s, Britain
became involved in and was affected by the international
economic crisis of 1929–33. The country began to recover in
1933 and during the 1930s the total British labour force rose by
17 per cent and the labour force within manufacturing industry
by 8 per cent. Industrial output increased by 23 per cent
between 1929 and 1937, but the volume of exports fell by a
further 13 per cent. It was the falling export markets which
were essentially responsible for difficulties in basic trades
throughout the 1930s. Nevertheless, terms of trade continued to
rise in Britain's favour enabling her real income to increase
despite the continual fall in exports. At the start of the Second
World War Britain was regaining her economic strength by
adapting her industrial structure. In no period in Britain's industrial history were circumstances so conducive to industrial
change as during the 1940s and the 1950s. The balance of
industrial power shifted and the inter-relationships between individual trades were revolutionized. The developments which
had most far-reaching effects were the emergence of the oil
refining and nuclear energy industries in which over £1,000
million was invested between 1945 and 1959. Overall, the
volume of industrial production in the United Kingdom rose by
72 per cent between 1938 and 1960. There is no one reason

for the rapid technological growth which has taken place since 1939 and for the new products, manufacturing processes and materials which have emerged. The greatest impetus was provided by the Second World War and the defence programme. So that it is true to say that the present progress could not have been achieved without government-sponsored research and the defence contracts.

The location of industry also changed drastically after the First World War—no longer was the location of a particular basic material the deciding factor in the choice of industrial sites. New and expanding industries grew up in areas other than those in which the declining industries were located, new industries were developing most rapidly in the South and in the Midlands. The industries in decay were the heavy industries while the newer industries were those which produced light finished consumer goods in neighbourhoods with the largest consumer markets, or centres with the best distributing facilities. Moreover, in place of skilled male labour most of the new industries required adaptable but essentially unskilled labour, much of which was female. The government made several attempts to deal with problems of the location of industry. At first efforts were geared towards encouraging and assisting migration from the depressed to the prosperous areas but later a policy to bring new industries to depressed areas was initiated. By the Special Areas Act of 1934 and subsequent legislation certain areas were selected to receive financial assistance and Commissioners were appointed to administer these measures. There was even an attempt to make the "Special Areas" more attractive to industrialists. The largest development in regional industrial planning occurred immediately after the Second World War when industry was more mobile than ever before. Between 1945 and 1948, 52 per cent of the total industrial building took place in the Development Areas, whereas between 1949 and 1955 the proportion was only 28 per cent.[1] Government intervention of this sort in the field of locational decisions was most significant for the future efficiency of British industry.

[1] G. C. Allen, *op. cit.*

Concurrently with economic and geographic changes following the First World War there were significant structural changes. One consequence of the technological developments was to increase the advantages of large-scale production and the highly capitalized firm. The Liberal Industrial Enquiry[1] of 1928 considered that the traditional competitive structure of British industry was no longer expedient and opinion was shifting to "controlled" competition, successfully practised in the new rayon, aluminium and dye stuffs industries. The First World War stimulated the growth of industrial combines: and, as was pointed out in the first chapter, competition was suppressed in the national interest while the government encouraged the setting up of industrial bodies to facilitate negotiations in the allocation of materials, import and export licensing, and the provision of loan capital. In 1916 the Federation of British Industries was established and by the end of the war there were more than 500 manufacturers' trade associations. Collective control was replacing isolated action and official support was given both to the unification movement in the chemical, electrical engineering and other industries and to the modernization of equipment and the standardization of products. Since the more efficient firms were most highly favoured by government contracts, they gradually enlarged their size and acquired a dominant share of the market, at the same time, early attempts at amalgamation, for instance in the cotton and shipbuilding industries, failed because they were insufficiently supported. Gradually between the wars, traditional antagonism to collective action was overcome, with the result that every basic industry was affected. Government intervention in the shape of financial assistance was often instrumental in the change of attitude. This period saw changes in ownership, extensive mergers, vast development in the scale and complexity of technology, the introduction of new, science-based industries, the extension of management sciences and the growth in influence of American companies.

[1]*Britain's Industrial Future,* Report of the Liberal Industrial Enquiry, London, 1928.

Ownership

There have been two phases in the shift of control in British industry. From the last century to this, the change was from the individual owner of a business to the less-clearly defined ownership of the large company. Since then, the structure of ownership and the effective control of industrial affairs has gradually become more centralized. Since 1900, legal forms have changed. In 1900, "the most common type of business organization was the unincorporated partnership or sole trader. The number of registered companies was . . . a mere 29,000", most of which were "private companies in the sense that they did not invite public subscription to their securities".[1] Today industry is conducted almost entirely by registered joint stock companies; there were 428,000 of these in 1962, when the number of public companies was 10,770. This legal change was symptomatic of an equally important economic change. In 1900 there were many large companies, but these seldom raised capital by public subscription and a large proportion of industrial output came from small and medium-sized firms directed by those who provided the capital. The growth of the very large company has meant a separation between ownership and control, a situation in which the shareholders can exert little influence on management and in which the managers form a professional salaried class. Nevertheless, "at least a quarter of the very large companies with over £3 million capital were in 1951 controlled directly or indirectly by the large shareholders".[2] And there are still a vast number of smaller concerns, including private companies, where ownership and control are one and the same.

G. M. Trevelyan points out that in the last half of the nineteenth century many old firms were replaced by the Limited Liability Company with a "bureaucracy of salaried managers".[3]

---

[1] L. C. B. Gower, "Business" in *Law and Opinion in England in the Twentieth Century* (ed. M. Ginsberg).

[2] P. Sargent Florence, "A New Enquiry into Ordinary Share Ownership", *The Times*, 12 August 1959.

[3] G. M. Trevelyan, *English Social History*, Longmans, 1944.

This was observed with unease not only by personnel who were to administer decisions, but also by some industrialists who felt that control of their business would be affected. Others saw dangers on the pseudo-religious level; that the managers would descend like a plague of locusts and nibble away at all large-scale operations. It can with firmness be said that there are some industrialists who think the same today! It was not only the growth in the use and number of managers which suggested a threat to the personal atmosphere of the industry of the period, but also the large scale manipulation of capital and industry meant an increase in the number and importance of share-holders. Trevelyan takes an over-pessimistic view of the share-holders' role, although part of this description cannot be denied: "the shareholder had no knowledge of the lives, thoughts or needs of the workmen employed by the Company". Limited liability made business a diarchy in which ownership and management were sharply differentiated and it encouraged absenteeism among shareholders who exercised ultimate cor-porate control but had no part in working operations.

Once the Limited Liability Company had become the basic structure for modern industry with a consequent over-all change in structure, there came a change in the control of power within the company. The shift in ownership was followed by a shift in control. The paid-up capital of registered joint stock com-panies with limited liability, the typical form of industrial enter-prise, rose from £2½ million in April 1914 to £4.1 million at the end of 1921 to over £6 million in 1938. The large increase between 1914 and 1921 was the result of war-time extensions, but it also reflected the share boom of 1919–20 when capital was increased by the ploughing back of the results of war-time profiteering and by speculative promotion at greatly inflated prices.[1] Much of this capital was lost again in the slump, but in the inter-war period the expansion of genuine joint-stock en-terprise continued and many individually owned firms and partnerships were converted to the joint stock form of organiza-

[1] Sidney Pollard, *The Development of the British Economy 1914-1950*, Edward Arnold, 1962.

tion. By 1938 the partnership or the individual businessman trading on his own had become quite exceptional in industry, though they could still be found in retail distribution, in agriculture and in the professions. The number of public joint stock companies on the register actually declined in this period, but at the same time there was a large increase in the number of private companies, as partnerships and even one-man firms registered to obtain the various benefits of the Company Acts. The private company, the typical form of organization for the family firm, was on the average much smaller than the public company.

The need for large sums of capital affected the extension of the joint stock type of organization. It developed fastest in industries composed of large firms and using a high proportion of capital per worker. The family firm gave way to the registered company with its numerous and anonymous shareholders and its elected Board of Directors. By the end of the 1930s one of the consequences of this development, the divorce of ownership from control, had become very marked. In most of the larger companies the proportion of the shares held by any single holder (including the Board) was insignificant and there were thousands of shareholders.

Apart from the single firm, the most widespread form of monopoly organization to arise between the wars was the trade association. There were very few of these before 1914, but they began to grow up quickly during the First World War. After the war the Committee on Trusts counted ninety-three associations among the many different industries with dealings with the Ministry of Munitions and thirty-five associations in the iron and steel industry. The Federation of British Industries, which began with fifty affiliated organizations in 1916, had 129 by 1918, mostly of the trade association type, with a membership of 16,000 firms with an aggregate capital of £4 million. Many of these trade associations collapsed in the slump of 1921–2 but in the "rationalization" movement of 1924–9, much of it government supported, others were formed. By the late 1930s there were one to two thousand in existence in manufacturing alone, with a similar number to be found in distribution and other spheres.[1]

The significant point to bear in mind is that the shift of ownership had many contributing and related causes and equally it had many important results in terms of the mechanics of a working system, for example it brought about changes in decision-making and produced the concept of the management team.

But the shift in ownership came as a response to a need within industry to change the basic structure. The change in ownership was not directly effected by government, the significance of which will emerge later in the study.

Scale and Complexity of Technology

The growth and the increasing complexity of technology has substantially influenced the nature of industry. Old industries have been modified by technological growth, involving for example the use of new methods to achieve the same ends, and technology has actually created many new industries, such as the synthetic fibre industry and the rubber and plastics industry. Between the wars Britain had to move from long dependence on the staple export industries to new industries requiring different skills and raw materials, and new locations, all aimed increasingly at a rising home market. During the inter-war years, the consumer was offered more new products and the industrialist more new machinery and materials than in any comparable period in history. As it was done without planning and with scarcely any understanding of its direction, it was done hesitantly, clumsily and expensively.

There was, nevertheless, a definite progressive development in the growth of technology from the time of the Industrial Revolution and there are some half-dozen influences related to technological advance which can be isolated. In the first place, there was the population increase. Paradoxically, it was the early technology—such as improved agricultural techniques which increased the food supply, rising standards of cleanliness,

[1]Sidney Pollard, *op. cit.*

advancing medical knowledge—which extended the life-span and reduced infant mortality, thus increasing the population; the increased population necessitated larger and more complex technology so that growth in both spheres combined during the nineteenth century in a mutually perpetuating relationship. The growth of population then stimulated the development of town life and technological advances, from the steam powered factory and gas-lighting to the steel framed skyscrapers and cinematography, spread most rapidly in an urban environment.

Apart from the necessities of war, various other factors contributed to technological development; the accumulation and international availability of capital, the impetus given by the growth of international trade, improvements in transport and communications, changes in Patent Law and the wider use of scientific and mathematic theory. Not only were these influences operating to affect technological growth in the nineteenth century, but it is development in precisely the same areas which affects industry today.

Technological development also brought specialization in industrial organization, that is, in the means of producing and distributing goods and services. The complex of techniques which in a modern concern begins with the production engineer or the chemical engineer, and continues through a series of specialists to end with the advertising agent and the market research team, were represented in the early stages of the industrial revolution by one or two men. Entrepreneurs like Josiah Wedgwood, Matthew Boulton, Benjamin Gott or Josiah Mason, for example, estimated some existing need or potential demand and moulded the machinery of production so as to provide for its satisfaction. Invention, technology, the factory system, even primitive forms of advertisements (like Wedgwood's famous catalogues) were instruments of their industrial development. As the nineteenth century proceeded, the number of those industries within which technology was the dynamic force increased. These included the engineering industry, the iron and steel industries and the chemical industry. Over the present century, technological progress has been so rapid that more than one-quarter of the goods produced in Europe today either did not exist fifty years ago or were only in the experimental stage of development; the aeroplane, penicillin and television are obvious examples. Existing wants are now being satisfied differently and sometimes in a diversity of ways; new materials and new methods of production make possible improvements in content, style and performance of products often at reduced cost. Stockings are made of nylon instead of silk, upholstery of plastic as well as leather, electric train coaches of aluminium as well as steel. The chemical and metallurgical industries have been responsible for the most innovation in recent years. The major advance of the last ten years in the UK has been the development of the petro-chemicals industry. The fact that such an industry has evolved has meant that other new materials have been developed, e.g. synthetic detergents, fertilizers and industrial solvents. In the metallurgical industry progress has been most marked in the sphere of alloys affecting primarily the engineering and vehicles industries.

Perhaps the most far-reaching effect of technological development is automation. (The term, which originated in the USA in 1936, means either "the automatic handling of parts between progressive production processes" or "the use of machines to control machines".[1]) The effect of automation deserves particular attention in this study as it has had specific and profound influence on the structure of industry and decision-making.

First it is necessary to make the distinction between mechanization and automation. The mechanization of a factory is a continuous process which evolves gradually as methods of production are changed piecemeal. Automated methods, on the other hand, have to be adopted to a certain minimum degree or not at all. Mechanization usually only affects labour at the point where the machine is introduced, whereas automation involves changes in factory lay-out and managerial responsibility. Furthermore automation often causes the limit in the ultimate growth of an enterprise to recede, for in manufacturing industries an enlargement in the scale of out-put first decreases

[1] J. H. Dunning and C. J. Thomas, *British Industry*, Hutchinson, 1966.

average costs and later increases them. One reason often given for this eventual increase in costs is the inability of top management to cope effectively with the increased responsibility and administration burden. The co-ordination of decision-making and policy-making is also likely to become less effective.[1] The very significant results of technological growth on work practices in industry will be considered in greater detail later in this chapter. The automation techniques of transfer processing, automatic assembly, control engineering and most recently computerization have had and are having far-reaching effects on labour, management, technologists themselves, on the skills required for jobs, on the use of capital and, interestingly, on the location of industry. For instance, a large degree of automation in a factory will cause a reduction in the numbers employed whilst not affecting output, which, if anything, increases. As a consequence, factories are likely to require less space and may be located on low value sites away from urban areas. Within the last two years ICI has established a unit costing nearly £11 million in the North East, yet offering employment to only one hundred people. With such a small number of personnel, there is no dependency on a large city or town to provide the labour force.

In the pattern of technological growth in recent times, there has been a considerable gap between invention and application. For instance, major new industries which emerged between 1919 and 1939 (electrical engineering, chemicals, rayon, radio, cinema, aircraft and motor engineering) were all based on inventions made in the generation before 1914, and the major discoveries of the inter-war years (television, the jet engine, nylon and penicillin) were not used practically in industry until after 1939. In fact, it was only in this period that part of British industry became interested in technological discovery itself and then primarily because of military needs. Most early government sponsorship (Department of Scientific and Industrial Research in 1916, The National Physical Laboratory, 1900 and the Medical Research Council in 1920) occurred before 1930

[1]These useful distinctions betwen mechanization and automation are made by J. H. Dunning and C. J. Thomas, *op. cit.*

and then declined in importance when private industry itself was turning to research and systematic control techniques to prove its methods and products. The effects, however, were uneven and half the industrial research expenditure was incurred in three industries, electrical engineering, chemicals, and aircraft, each with strong military associations. The Balfour Committee found that research in British firms was inadequate when compared with American firms.

The methods of technical progress are important, for progress has been achieved by the gradual adaptation and improvement, often of only humble parts of machines or materials, the linked development of one new process waiting for improvements in others before it can be applied, and the constant pressure on the average firm to install machines already in existence. In other words technological progress has been achieved not by spectacular brain-waves, but by gradual, controlled and guided experiment. The actual idea behind an invention has no significance for investment or industry until it has passed through the difficult and costly stage of development. The fact has intensified both the concentration of production in large firms and also the growing participation of the government in industrial research. The National Research Development Corporation's sponsorship of the Hovercraft is an example of government contribution to the development and design of an invention. Finally, technical progress has affected entrepreneurship, itself affecting the management of men, the lay-out of the plant, grouping, selection and training of staff, as well as work study and the study of fatigue.

American Company Influence

So far the aspects of industrial development which exerted their strongest influence on British industry up to 1950 have been considered. Since then the influences of the American company have been of major importance and have usually been of two kinds. In one respect the American company has served as a model to be imitated by industry in this country, but it has also been influential by its actual physical and geographic location in

*

Britain. The first are indirect influences and the second is of a more direct nature.

Historically, mechanized mass production in the United States, under the pressure of labour shortages, was introduced much earlier than in Britain. With the abundance of raw materials and the shortage of skilled labour, the evolution of American business was naturally characterized by a strong labour-saving tendency. Mass production was used to create a mass-consumption market which operated under competitive conditions and which continued in spite of monopolistic tendencies. Anti-trust legislation in the United States is one of the indications of the central position of business in American life and of the American government's concern to protect business. Competitive conditions made rationalization of resources necessary at an early date so that management techniques, standardization and the division of labour became prominent. Then when United States business emerged from its isolation after the Second World War, it brought with it a business system geared to the handling of a strongly competitive mass market with a high degree of product diversity. The foundation of the American industrial system is mass production at low production costs per unit and with high wages. The concept of mass production for a mass market and recognition of wages as the predominant market force are basically market-oriented and as such, are essentially different from those which have dominated European business development.

American business in Europe and the influence exercised by American business literature and business schools have been increasing since 1950 and particularly since the formation of the European Economic Community (EEC), in which American private capital used for direct investment has tripled since 1957.[1] The direct economic influence of American operations has stimulated competition, but has also, when there has been too much reliance on the American firm, led to insufficient research initiative. The indirect influence has also been very important.

[1] M. van der Haas, *The Enterprise in Transition: an Analysis of European and American Practice,* Tavistock Publications, 1967.

Both American business and the American budget are geared to achievement; whereas in Britain a cost-budget is often restrictive and the employee has budget responsibility, in the United States the employee has achievement responsibilty. Again the American tendency—often contrary to the European one—is usually to make decisions after exhaustive enquiries on matters both central and incidental to the main issue, and to try to open up values for analysis, as illustrated by the development of professional management.

Another way in which American manufacturing firms in Europe have exercised their influence on work practices is in the degree of control they assume over work contracted out to European firms, demanding full information and sometimes alteration on every aspect of the job from floor organization up. Professionalism as a characteristic of American business is also having its effect on business and education in Europe. All in all, the American company influence on British industry, especially compared with other basic influences, is in its infancy and the total outcome, as well as specific effects, will have to await the passing of time before they can be accurately assessed.

Science-based Industries

An examination of the science-based industries follows naturally from the question of the scale and complexity of technology. Furthermore, a consideration of the science-based industries requires a study of particular industries. Scientific research was at first regarded as a supplementary aid to productivity improvement, but now is increasingly being recognized as the basis of industrial progress and improved living standards. What have been referred to already as the new industries (those which have been replacing steel, in importance) are generally also the science-based industries.

The electrical engineering industry is perhaps the most important of these industries and may be regarded as the symbol of new industrial Britain. This industry was technically backward in 1918, but in 1930 was competing internationally as a result of, for example, improved technical and thermal efficiency, falling prices of coal, the closing of high-cost stations and the British "grid". Perhaps next in importance in the new industries has been the motor industry. The motor car has changed people's habits of living, affected the lay-out of towns, created the first conveyor-belt factories and stimulated many ancillary industries such as oil refining, rubber, electrical goods, glass, metallurgy and mechanical engineering. Closely linked with the development of the motor car engine have been developments in aircraft production.

Some new industries have been based on advance in the science of chemistry and in chemical engineering, foremost of these being the man-made fibre industry, limited before 1939 almost entirely to rayon. This particular industry was dominated from the beginning by a small number of large firms such as Courtauld's and British Celanese. The chemical industry came to include the production of explosives and dyestuffs, heavy chemicals, industrial gases, fertilizers, medical chemicals and plastics. Outstanding in the chemical industry has been Imperial Chemical Industries Limited (ICI), founded in 1926 by a merger of four companies. There has been remarkable progress in the field of glass-making, both in ornamental and optical glass. Glass-making is an example of an old industry being revolutionized by new techniques, but such processes as the working of aluminium, rubber and plastic typify new industries based on new materials. The plastics industry dates from the invention of "bakelite" in 1908, but was not an established industry until the 1930s. Considerable progress has been made in the area of consumer goods and products such as boots and shoes, hosiery, flour milling and the canning, freezing and packaging of foods. As indicated earlier, developments in these science-based industries were neither spontaneous nor isolated. It was a gradual process of development, and discovery in one industry being adapted for use in another.

Just as there is a need within firms to ensure rapid communication of ideas and co-ordination of research work in production and sales departments, so too can co-operation between firms produce beneficial results. Technologically, modern industry is essentially integrated and inter-related; but to reap the maximum benefit from technical improvements, efficient and continuous communication between specialist and management must take place. Responsibility for the successful application of science and technology to industry is essentially a question of management receptivity and efficiency. The integration of research activities with the production and sales programme and the assurance of good communication facilities between the various departments is needed if valuable ideas are not to be lost. Efficient methods of publicizing the results of basic research are also needed if scientific advances are to have their full effect on industrial progress. For the communication of results from scientist to scientist, the existing methods are satisfactory so long as they keep pace with the growth in volume of scientific work and so long as there is adequate abstracting to keep the individual scientist's reading within manageable proportions.

The part which government can play in guiding and stimulating the use of advanced technology and new processes will be seen when the structure of government is examined and, in particular, that of the Ministry of Technology.

Work-practices: The Results of Industrial Development

All of the aspects of industrial development thus far considered—the change in ownership and control, the growth of technology and the American company influence—have had considerable effect on work practices in British industry. One of the first results, largely arising from changes in ownership and technological growth, was the trend towards rationalization, the term by which much of the reorganization of British industry in the inter-war years was popularly known. Rationalization has been defined as "an industrial combination not to secure monopolistic advantages, but to secure economies of production and distribution" or "a process necessary to produce higher organization rather than to confer monopolistic advantages".[1] The

[1] J. H. Dunning and C. J. Thomas, British Industry, op. cit.

aim of the inter-war reconstruction schemes, many of which were sponsored by the government, was to raise industrial efficiency in an effort to eliminate excess capacity, improve production methods, introduce systematic work specialization, and encourage the economies of concentrated management, distribution and research. The actual form and extent of rationalization varied according to individual circumstances, but there were two main features common to the schemes adopted, which usually had government support. In the first place, prices were fixed and production regulated by such methods as price maintenance, the use of boycotts and exclusive dealing. Secondly, an attempt was made to raise the efficiency of production by replacing obsolete equipment and amalgamation. The aims were generally to effect greater central control amongst firms and in some instances there was complete financial unification. For example, the government lent its support to monopolistic arrangements to improve the financial position of industry. The cartelization of the coal industry under the Coal Mines Act 1930; the establishment in the same industry of central selling schemes in 1936; the strengthening of monopoly in the iron and steel industry after the formation of the British Iron and Steel Federation in 1932; the measures, culminating in the Cotton Industry (Reorganization) Act of 1939 to reduce competition in the cotton industry; the support given to rationalization schemes in the shipbuilding, tinplate, wool-combing and other industries; the monopolistic producers' boards set up under the Agricultural Marketing Acts; the restriction of road competition with the railways imposed under the Road and Rail Traffic Act of 1933 are not only examples of government assistance in rationalization schemes, but also indicate a retreat from competition in British industry between the wars and the government policy of fostering that movement.[1] In fact, the policy did little to relieve unemployment or to promote the redistribution of resources which the changed economic position of the country required.

[1] G. C. Allen, *op. cit.*

Industrial Change and Labour

The effect of the change in ownership on the workers—the increasing separation between the owner and the worker and the consequent replacement of the owner by the manager or the management team—has been considered. Technological growth also had a profound effect on the position of the employee. With increasing automation for example, there has been the fear that there will be severe and prolonged unemployment as a consequence. This is not entirely unfounded but in the long run experience has shown that automation and increasing mechanization are more likely to raise living standards and bring about shorter hours of work. Also if industry thought that automation would result in an excessively high level of unemployment, it would, in effect be courting its own downfall. The degree and length of unemployment in industry due to technological change will depend on the general level of employment and the ease with which labour can move between different occupations, industries and areas. Automation is a net investment, consequently the demand for labour in the capital goods industries is likely to increase. Also the reduction in the length of the working week, considered to be one of the benefits of automation, would mean an increase in the demand for service industries, such as transport and entertainment.

A very specific result of technological change and automation is the change in the industrial skills required. An increasing number of people, for example, will be required for employment on maintenance work, and they will generally need to be high-grade technicians with advanced technical training.

Industrial Change and the Director

The board of directors is the link in the joint stock company between shareholders and the operating staff; it is the managing director who is the link between shareholders and employees in most large companies. The following diagram shows the overlapping relationship between the three groups of persons and bodies within the company organization associated with the

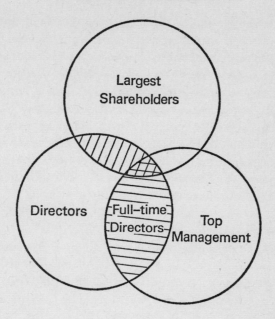

activities of top control and decision-making. The largest share-holders are identical to some extent with directors and are shown to intersect, but top management and directors intersect still more, as represented by the full-time managing directors. The seat of control is very likely to be somewhere in the intersections as shaded in the diagram. The most likely persons to be in control are those who are both large shareholders *and* directors, or directors *and* top managers.[1] The important point, however, is that control now rests with a combination of different types of people in the company hierarchy.

The activities of the directors of a company are diverse. They decide the rate of dividend to be declared on the ordinary shares. (Shareholders may reduce, but not increase the rate.) They propose any new capital structure such as the issue of shares on the market, bonus shares, preference shares or deben-tures. They review and check up on the work of management

[1] P. Sargent Florence, *Ownership, Control and Success of Large Companies,* Sweet and Maxwell, London, 1961.

and they question management, a job in which the outside
part-time director plays a special role. They form the link
between different companies by holding directorships in more
than one company. They appoint top managers, determine the
salaries of the top managers, organize new posts at the top of the
management structure and decide on general lines of policy such
as what to make, how much and at what price with what investment. In this specific area, however, subject to the control
he is able to acquire, the managing director is probably more
important than the board of directors, for it is he who interprets
the broad directives from the board.

Industrial Change and Management

With the increasing complexity of processes, managerial
control becomes more exacting and involves an ever-increasing
number of managers, supervisors and technicians. For example,
in the Ford engine plant at Cleveland, Ohio, where the degree
of automation is extensive, there is one foreman to eighteen
operatives, whereas at the Detroit plant, which is less advanced
technologically, the ratio is one to thirty-one. In a certain British
steel-making firm, the change-over to a continuous strip mill
process resulted in almost a 50 per cent increase in the number
of managers, supervisors, clerical workers and technicians. The
role of the manager in these new conditions changes drastically.
Techniques which were the prerogative of the managing director
of twenty-five years ago must be understood by the junior
manager today. Operational research, methods study, human
relations, budgetary control and production planning have all
graduated from the Harvard Business School to the factory
floor.

Management today is a three-stage process consisting of
policy-making, supervision, and techniques. Many people find
it difficult to distinguish between supervision and management
yet we have now noted that the former is a part of management
as a whole. The responsibilities of a supervisory job are the
control of work and workers, the discharge of orders from
management and the interpretation of policy at the shop floor

level. The modern manager must know the dynamics within
his organization. He must recognize whether he is working in an
organization which has no defined structure and vary his tactics
in relation to his superior, subordinates and peers respectively.
The manager has a greater need for administrative and social
skills than ever before; he will need to spend more time on
planning and formulating objectives, on liaison, in communi-
cating with people and in co-ordinating the efforts of others. To
sum up: the changing role of the manager in industry involves
him more and more in the establishing of firm objectives and in
the making of plans to achieve them. There are management
tools to help in this important task which are referred to in
detail elsewhere.[1]

The Trade Unions

No study of industry would be complete without a consideration of the structure and development of the trade unions. The
history of trade unionism is particularly significant in the context
of this study, since it illustrates both the reasons why government was forced to take an interest in industrial affairs in the
nineteenth century, and the way in which that interest was
turned into action.

The earliest unions, the Guilds, were essentially domestic
bodies concerned with status and "pride in the job". They were
responsible for protecting the standards of their crafts by fixing
prices, by defining apprenticeship terms, and by determining
the piece-rate to be paid to journeymen. But they had no power
to strike: any combination of members of Guilds to enforce
their views was liable to be punished under the common law
as "conspiracy in restraint of trade".

The Guild structure had, however, broken down during the
rise of capitalism in the seventeenth century—it was, essentially,
an association of equals and not relevant to the new relationship
of employer and employee. New industrial conditions made
Guilds and wage regulation obsolete, and Parliament, having

[1]For a more detailed study, see Eric Moonman, *The Manager and the
Organization,* Tavistock Publications, London, 1961.

given up any attempt to satisfy the demands of the journeymen, allowed a state of *laissez-faire* to prevail in the labour market.

Combinations, however, whether between masters or men, were still forbidden. The first attempts to by-pass the effect of the law came in the eighteenth century with the rise of the Friendly Societies. Founded primarily to enable members to help themselves and each other in periods of sickness and unemployment, discussions between members led to agitation for better working conditions. This led to the growth of the "trade clubs" —local organizations of people working in a particular craft in a particular place—and their activities so alarmed the Government (ever mindful of the French Revolution) that the common law was reinforced with the Combination Acts of 1799 and 1800, which made working-class organizations illegal and laid the Trade Clubs open to charges of conspiracy. Many members were transported, but the Clubs continued to flourish in some localities.

This situation continued for the next twenty-five years, during which time pioneers such as Robert Owen, Francis Place and William Lovett worked on behalf of the labouring and artisan classes, helping them to gain experience in association and collective self-help. A new consciousness of needs and rights developed, and Joseph Hume, a Radical MP, was able to persuade the government that the Trade Clubs no longer represented a threat. The Combination Acts were repealed in 1824 as a result, but this was immediately followed by a wave of militant union action brought on by the depression of 1825, so that a further Act was passed limiting the activities of the unions to negotiation. In spite of this, the next ten years witnessed a rapid growth of trade unions; the most ambitious—though somewhat premature—venture was Robert Owen's Grand National Consolidated Trade Union, which had over half-a-million members but only lasted a year or two. It collapsed after the affair of the "Tolpuddle Martyrs", when six members of a branch of the Union were prosecuted for "administering oaths".

The Chartist Movement, although primarily political, also gave impetus to the development of trade unionism in the first half of the nineteenth century. But the significant growth of the movement to the position it occupies today occurred rather quietly between 1850 and 1870, when a wider distribution of wealth, better working conditions, and a higher standard of living prevailed. The need for labour organization simply paralleled the growth in industry, trade and communications generally, and it was on the basis of the prosperity of these twenty years that trade unionism, the Co-operative Movement, and other organizations developed.

Unions founded in this period include the Miners' Association, formed in 1841, the National Association of United Trades for the Protection of Labour, in 1845, and the Amalgamated Society of Engineers in 1851. The first embryonic trades union congress met in Manchester in 1868, and by the time Gladstone formed his first government, trade unionism was an established feature of industrial life, though one still greatly restricted by unfavourable legislation.

The Trade Union Act of 1871 finally recognized the trade unions and made them legal, but their activities were severely restricted by the Criminal Law Amendment Act of the same year. This Act was repealed in 1875 when the right of peaceful picketing was restored, and remaining restrictions were removed by the Trade Union Amendment Act of 1876.

The next attack on union freedom came from the House of Lords in its judicial capacity, with the *Taff Vale* case in 1901; the judgement was reversed by Act of Parliament in 1906, when the Trade Disputes Act gave immunity from damages arising out of trade disputes; again in 1909, the *Osborne* judgement declared the use of union funds for political purposes illegal—and again the judgement was reversed by Act of Parliament. The same course was followed after the decision in *Rookes v. Barnard* in 1964.

Throughout the last quarter of the nineteenth century the unions gathered numerical strength and staged successful strikes —of employees at Bryant and May, of gas workers and of dockers, for example, all in 1889—and the trend continued until the end of the 1914–18 war. The need to maintain production meant that the co-operation of the unions was essential and the war left them relatively strong, but the depression of the 1920s and the General Strike of 1926 undermined their position which was further weakened by the Trade Disputes Act of 1927 restricting their activities in some directions.

Since then, the number of union members has steadily increased, until, at the end of 1966, they totalled some ten million. The actual number of unions, however, has fallen by nearly half since the beginning of the century.

The unions as they are today are a very different proposition from the nineteenth and early twentieth century combines directed towards obtaining the barest minimum in the way of a fair deal from the employers. Their aims have diversified as industry has developed, changing the requirements of workers as a result. The unions are still concerned with the welfare of employees but, as the aims of labour and management have become less polarized, the industrial relationship between trade union and management levels has changed correspondingly.

The changes in the nature and structure of industry described earlier in this chapter have brought many problems to the trade unions. One of the most difficult has been the question of communications : where both the size of an industry and the unions represented in its work-force have made communications between the rank and file and the union leadership difficult, the shop stewards have become the main spokesmen for the employees, a trend not always welcomed by either the union leadership or by management.

The resistance of some unions in some industries to the modernization of work practices has led to clamorous, though not necessarily widely supported, demands that the unions be brought under control. The early stages of the debate about the power of the unions and their role in the modern industrial scene led to the setting up in 1965 of the Royal Commission on Trade Unions and Employers' Organizations, which reported in June 1968.[1]

[1] *The Donovan Report*, Cmnd. 3623.

The Royal Commission recommended the establishment of an Industrial Relations Commission which would study and make proposals on a wide range of industrial disputes, other than wage disputes, but having no legal power to enforce its recommendations; it also suggested that there should be a Registrar for the trade unions, whose job would be to record and advise on the rule-books and procedures of trade unions; also the establishment of a review body to hear appeals from individuals who have complaints against a trade union on questions of membership, and of a series of regional tribunals to hear cases of unfair dismissals. It thus resisted the various pressures and demands for bringing the unions under greater legal control.

The government implemented the recommendations of the Donovan Report to the extent of setting up an Industrial Relations Commission under the chairmanship of George Woodcock, former General Secretary of the TUC: the Commission produced its first reports early in 1970.

Despite the non-legalistic suggestions of the Donovan Commission, the government thought it necessary to attempt a legal solution to the problem of the unions' failure to control unofficial strikes, and there ensued the long and hard-fought campaign in the first half of 1969 over "penal sanctions".

The battle revealed, above all, the inability of a government to identify with industrial life and experience. This was partly due to the composition of the Cabinet at that time. At the height of the debate in the Parliamentary Labour Party the Cabinet were strategically ordered to appear on the platform in Committee Room 14 in the House of Commons. A show of solidarity was considered by the Whips' Office to be essential. The Secretary of State made an unconvincing attempt to persuade the MPs present to back her, finally deploying the argument, and incidentally quashing any rumours that had been circulating, that "there was no disagreement in the Cabinet on the need for penal clauses". Barbara Castle's great oratorical skill and inimitable manner can normally be relied on to capture an audience, myself included, but on this occasion few were listening to her, for our attention was directed to the Cabinet, neatly assembled alongside her. It had occurred to most of us that, with only two exceptions, the industrial or commercial experience of the twenty Cabinet members present could be measured in days, and those presumably spent in casual visits.

Another crucial factor was the campaign conducted throughout the country by the trade union movement—even the less militant unions like my own, the National Graphical Association, were stung into action and demanded that the penal clauses be rejected. The Labour Party itself was active; both inside and outside Parliament. Indeed they were more strongly roused by this question than by any other in the whole of the Parliament.

In my opinion, the turning point was reached when all this pressure turned the issue into one of confidence in the Prime Minister. Had the government persisted in its attempts to introduce an Industrial Relations Bill with penal clauses it would almost certainly have brought about the downfall of the Prime Minister.

I was among the leaders of one campaign to defeat the Bill, but there was another, parallel, campaign to get rid of the Prime Minister. The two campaigns were kept separate because of the determination that they should remain so on the part of the industrial action group, of which I was chairman. But it is quite clear that time was running out fast and, had the government proposal for penal sanctions not collapsed at the eleventh hour, the two factions would almost certainly have merged.

It is difficult to describe the feelings of determination of Labour MPs at this time, but they really were tough and implacable. In the end, Barbara Castle was thrown to the wolves; but it could so easily have been the Prime Minister himself.

Conclusions

The nature and structure of industry have changed profoundly since the beginning of the century. Management has, perhaps, adapted to the changes more readily than labour—but then, commercial necessity has probably forced them to face up to change more readily.

Specifically, there has been a transition from production centred business to product or market centred business. As a result of this, selling is being upgraded to a systematic process with more emphasis on market research, sales forecasting and sales promotion by specialized personnel.

The transition from owner control to professional management has been the most far-reaching change. Today most people are employed by a corporation endowed by law with separate and independent existence, such as a joint stock company, local authority, nationalized industry or the like, whose business is conducted and managed by individuals acting for them. These people will more often than not be employees themselves, but as "management" they will settle the terms and conditions of employment within their organizations by negotiation either with the employees themselves or with trade union representatives on their behalf. If industry is going to continue to be adaptable to change, the managers and union leaders must not be content to fulfil their roles in the traditional manner, but must be prepared to innovate.

3

THE STRUCTURE OF GOVERNMENT

"THE COMPLETE ACT of government consists of the conversion of the desires or will of some individuals or groups into the behaviour of others or all in the society in which they dwell. . . . The purpose of the government is to convert all such desire or will into the authorized and commanded behaviour of those who live or are of that settlement we call the 'state'. The desire or will may emanate from one mind, or spring spontaneously from many, or be developed by a minority."[1]

As every schoolchild is taught, in Britain government derives from an unwritten constitution which is both a limited monarchy and a parliamentary democracy which changes rapidly. The constitutional approach has its limitations, however. It ignores the responsibility of the electorate for the quality of its politicians, and encourages both ignorance of and indifference to the real nature of politics. A more relevant approach is that of the irreverent Max Nicholson, "Government is the exercise of authority, and of the power which should accompany it".[2] Politics is about power : Tory governments have always understood this, the Labour Party has been slow to recognize and make use of it.

The exercise of authority by "government" covers a wide range of controls, from Cabinet level down to local councils.[3] This chapter is mainly concerned with the organization of government at Whitehall, while at a later stage the role of the

[1]Herman Finer, *The Theory and Practice of Modern Government*, Methuen, 1961.
[2]Max Nicholson, *The System: The Misgovernment of Modern Britain*. Hodder, 1967.
[3]David Price, MP, Industrial and Educational Research Foundation, Conference, London, July 1969.

Civil Service will be considered. We shall not, unless specifically stated, be concerned with local authority functions or staff, public boards or nationalized industries.

The pattern of contemporary government may perhaps be seen more accurately after a study of its history and influence.

The 1832 and 1867 Reform Acts to extend the franchise were both closely related to the new forms of wealth based on manufacturing and commerce, which had grown out of the Industrial Revolution. The Whigs in the 1830s realized that industrialists and merchants, the new industrial equivalent of the landed property element in British society, must be represented in Parliament. The Conservative reform in 1867 extended the principles laid down in 1832. The period between the two Reform Acts witnessed a continuing shift in population to the big industrial towns and a further redistribution of parliamentary seats was required. The Act of 1867 increased the middle-class vote in the counties and extended the vote to artisans and the better-off workers in the towns. Universal suffrage, the original aim of the reformers of the 1830s, was not of course achieved until 1928, when the Act of 1918 removed all the anomalies in male franchise and extended the vote to the majority of women. The history of parliamentary reform between 1828–1928 shows the strengthening of democracy in the triumvirate structure of monarch, Parliament and electorate in the British government, through the growth and increasing strength of the electorate.

The machinery of government responsible for the "exercise of authority and power" has, like the electorate, undergone considerable changes in structure since the beginning of the nineteenth century. As might be expected, the actual composition of the Commons changed as the Reform Bills were passed, though the process was a slow one. In 1833 there were 217 Members of Parliament who were sons of peers or baronets; in 1860 there were 180 and in 1880 there were still 170. Further consequences of the extension of suffrage were the ending of the influence of the Crown on Parliament, and the displacement by the House of Commons of the House of Lords as the centre of political influence. Ultimately, the result of this process of democratization was that collective ministerial responsibility became a political necessity. Hans Daalder[1] describes the change in the machinery of government in the nineteenth century as a shift first from Crown to Commons and to Common Law, and then a further shift to Cabinet, Constituencies and Civil Service. Mr. Daalder points out that today the Cabinet virtually dominates the legislative process since it determines the main lines of policy and formulates the budget; Parliamentary government has thus become Cabinet government. This book is concerned primarily with the Cabinet, as the decision-making body (including non-Cabinet departments and ministries), and with the Civil Service, as the supplier of information for the basis of decisions and as the body charged with carrying them out.

The British Cabinet grew out of secret meetings of important court officials called "Great Officers of State" and "Principal Secretaries to the King". Over the centuries these offices moved out of Court and, as parliamentary power increased, the Crown had to fill these Cabinet positions with people with parliamentary influence. As a result of the setting up of new government departments to deal with particular needs during the nineteenth century, the Cabinet grew in number and became more formalized in structure. From five members in 1783 to ten or eleven in the early nineteenth century, the Cabinet grew to fourteen or fifteen around 1850, seventeen by the end of the nineteenth century and more than twenty under Asquith in 1915. This expansion was partly the result of administrative requirements: the Cabinet was the centre for arbitrating interdepartmental disputes and because discussions were secret and informal and no minutes were taken, it was necessary for all Ministers to be present to be fully informed of decisions affecting their departments.

The divisions of government power which most closely relate to the structure of decision-making today, occurred in the latter half of the nineteenth century. The Privy Council was, at first, the repository of every kind of new duty of supervision

[1]Hans Daalder, *Cabinet Reform in Britain, 1914-1963*, Stanford: Oxford, 1964.

over public services. Its functions could be classified alphabetically: "It was responsible for assizes, burial boards, charters of boroughs, clergy returns, coinage currency, contagious diseases of animals, convocation and so on to the end of the alphabet."[1] It is obvious that with the rapid development of modern industrial society, with all its social and economic implications, traditional offices in the government structure, like the Privy Council, absorbed new responsibilities on an *ad hoc* basis. The Home Office is another example of this omnibus allocation of general responsibility, from the enforcement of the regulations of the early Factory Acts, control of industrial diseases and the manufacture of explosives to the protection of wild flowers and control of advertisements and money-lenders.

A major tendency of administrative development in the nineteenth century was the formation of special Boards to take over duties performed by the Privy Council and Home Office. By 1820 the Board of Trade was well established, and in 1851 a Board of Works was set up in charge of construction and maintenance of palaces, parks and public buildings. Another illustration was the establishment in 1871 of the post of President of the Local Government Board. This was to consolidate into one Department numerous government functions, particularly in the fields of poor law and public health, which had previously been carried out by the Privy Council, Home Secretary and Poor Law Board.

A further development was the evolution of a number of Departments in existence today out of nineteenth-century Departments. The Ministry of Housing and Local Government provides an interesting and pertinent example of departmental development. Between 1871 and 1919 the main control over local authorities was vested in the Local Government Board. The Ministry of Health took over these responsibilities until 1951 when it had the enormous task of administering the National Health Service. Its local government responsibilities were therefore transferred to the Ministry of Town and Country

[1] K. B. Smellie, *A Hundred Years of English Government*, Duckworth, second edition 1950.

Planning (a war-time innovation) under the new title of Local Government and Planning, the name being changed in 1951 to the Ministry of Housing and Local Government. Again, the development of specific departmental responsibility as outlined above emphasizes the essentially arbitrary allocation of responsibility.

Of equal importance with the setting up of Boards and Departments was the tendency to grant wider discretionary powers to Ministers and their Departments. From 1870 onwards details of bills were decided departmentally.

One of the most important changes in the concept of government administration was brought about by the First World War —a change in the structure of the Cabinet. Before the war all government Departmental Ministers were represented on the Cabinet for the reasons outlined earlier. During the war, because of increased activity and the creation of new departments, this system was unwieldy and the representation of Ministers on the Cabinet was limited. Certain Departments took on greater importance, at least temporarily: for example, the War Office, the newly-created Ministry of Munitions, the Ministry of Food, and the Committee of Imperial Defence.

The major landmark in any consideration of the machinery of British Government was the Ministry of Reconstruction Report of the Machinery of Government (known as the Haldane Committee Report) which appeared in 1918. The Committee was appointed in July 1917 to "enquire into the responsibilities of the various Departments of the central executive Government, and to advise in what manner the exercise and distribution by the Government of its functions should be improved". The Committee intended to define the general principles which should govern the distribution of responsibility and to illustrate its application. The Committee stated:

Our investigations . . . have made it evident to us that there is much overlapping and consequent obscurity and confusion in the functions of the Departments of executive Government. This is largely due to the fact that many of these Departments have been gradually evolved in compliance with current needs, and that the purposes for which they were thus called into being have gradually so altered that the later stages of the process have not accorded in principle with those that were reached earlier. In other instances Departments appear to have been rapidly established without preliminary insistence on definition of function and precise assignment of responsibility. Even where Departments are most free from these defects, we find that there are important features in which the organization falls short of a standard which is becoming progressively recognized as the foundation of efficient action.

This statement, which was the summation of the Committee's inquiry in 1918, is still so relevant to existing difficulties in government structure as to provide the most accurate definition of present-day problems.

The Haldane Committee made a number of apposite recommendations regarding the Cabinet structure. Among these were the suggestions that the Cabinet should be small in number, perhaps consisting of ten to twelve persons; that it should meet frequently; that it should be supplied with information and material necessary to arrive at expeditious decisions; that it should personally consult with all Ministers whose work was likely to be affected by Cabinet decisions; and that it should have a systematic method of ensuring that its decisions were effectually carried out. It went on to suggest the main divisions into which the government ought to be divided and which ought to be represented on the Cabinet. These were Finance, National Defence, External Affairs, Research and Information, Production, Transport and Commerce, Employment, Supplies, Education, Health and Justice. Many of these recommendations were acted upon, although departmental interests prevented the total rationalization of government structure. Although Ministers in the Cabinet represent only a portion of the total Ministries and Departments, they number twenty or more rather than the ten or twelve recommended by Haldane.

The divisions into which government activities should be

organized continued to be more numerous than those suggested, and, as government extended its activities into new fields, have been further augmented. The autumn of 1969, however, saw what appears to be an end to the diversification of Ministries, in the creation of two "super-Ministries" (to borrow the Press jargon). The activities of the Department of State for Local Government and Regional Planning do not concern us here, but a review of the role, past as well as present, of the Ministry of Technology is essential, for it is largely in the hands of this Ministry that the future of the partnership between government and industry lies.

The Ministry of Technology was set up in 1964, and by the beginning of 1968 had assumed responsibility for the following areas of public business: responsibility for the Government's relationship with the engineering and vehicles industries, the so-called "sponsorship" function; merchant shipbuilding, with responsibility for carrying out the Geddes Report's proposed reconstruction of the industry; the Atomic Energy Authority; Government Research Establishments and the National Research Development Corporation; the government's relationship with the aircraft and aerospace industries; and government procurement of defence aircraft and defence electronics, and all that goes with them. It also has responsibility for fostering general technological advances.

During the first five years of its existence, under the direction of, first, Frank Cousins, and then Anthony Wedgwood Benn as its Ministers, the Ministry abandoned the idea that "science" should be kept at bay from the main government machine in order to preserve the integrity of research, and became actively involved in bringing industry and government research establishments together in order to get the best possible cross-fertilization of ideas and markets. To quote Wedgwood Benn, "Our number one mission is to use technology to cure Britain's balance of payments problem." The Permanent Secretary to the Ministry, Sir Richard Clarke, put it somewhat less tersely: "We see our task as being to sharpen public awareness of the

THE STRUCTURE OF GOVERNMENT

decisive position of industrial technology and productive efficiency in the attainment of all our national objectives."

Either way, the almost total success of the Ministry in achieving its aims has encouraged the Prime Minister to think that it can now take on responsibility for industry on an even wider basis. The Ministry of Technology has, as a result of the restructuring announced on 5 October 1969, taken over the functions of the Ministry of Power and the industrial functions of both the Board of Trade and of the Department of Economic Affairs. The Ministry thus acquires responsibility for the greater part of private and public industry, for decisions concerning the location of industry, for investment grants, regional economic development and the industrial Reorganization Corporation.

This redistribution of functions is a logical one. It leaves the Board of Trade free to concentrate its energies on overseas trade and export promotion, commercial policies and services such as civil aviation and insurance. The size of the new Ministry of Technology should make it strong enough to check the Treasury from exercising too rigid a control over finance, and the bringing of all industrial functions under one Ministry should lead to some saving in the time spent in inter-departmental disputes. Whether this will work out in practice depends on two factors: whether the Minister is strong enough to make the unity as much a reality as Mr. Healey has done with the integration of the Service Departments in the Ministry of Defence; and on the quality of the 30,000 civil servants under his command. On the first point we shall just have to wait and see; the second question will be considered after the history of interaction between government and industry has been examined.

This latest development is a reversal of the general trend in British administration, which, to quote G. M. Young, "was made by administrators throwing out their lines until they met and formed a system".[1] The pattern of government as it exists today is the result of piecemeal development over the last

[1]G. M. Young, *Victorian England: Portrait of an Age,* Oxford, second edition, 1953.

hundred years, when the allocation of responsibility has been made on the basis of the needs of the moment as they arose without any thought for long-term planning or consequences. Their defects in this approach were made apparent by the Haldane Report; if the changes in government structure of October 1969 really do represent a conscious attempt to stream-line that structure they have come about none too soon.

Finally, it is important when using the term "government" not to think only in abstract terms and not to ignore the political ideologies which have always affected the way governments behave. Whilst the permanent Civil Service, the basis of govern-ment in the abstract sense, has provided the constant and long-term framework for relations with industry, those relations have been most dramatically affected by the identification of the Conservative Party with capital and of Socialism with labour. The history of government involvement with industry has run parallel to the history of the rise and fall of the two Parties in Parliament. Yet, as we shall see, this is less obviously the case today.

4

INTERACTION OF GOVERNMENT
AND INDUSTRY

THE PROTAGONISTS AND their functions are identified. A critical question remains : how do they interact, both in the past and in the present, and is there any underlying philosophy behind government's involvement with industry?

"In all the more advanced communities the great majority of things are worse done by the intervention of government, than the individuals most interested in the matter would do them, or cause them to be done."[1] Thus wrote John Stuart Mill, the political economist, in the heady days of the industrial revolution, about the mid-nineteenth century.

Just over a hundred years later, Political and Economic Planning—an independent study group—commented on the industrial scene : "Neither of the main political parties denies that a degree of intervention is necessary, however they may disagree on its extent and the methods used."[2] The wheel has come full circle from the classic Victorian doctrine of *laissez-faire* to a view that modern industry is so complex in its structure, so dependent on massive injections of capital for re-equipment, and so powerful in the way it impinges on everyday life, that it cannot be left entirely to the men who run it or the shareholders who own it.

The growth of this view has not been as steady as some observers have sought to make out. Its genesis was cyclical, subject to spurts forward and sudden reversals. The supporters of a greater role for the state in industry under-estimated the vigour of the old mercantile attitudes, while the tenacious

[1]J. S. Mill, *The Principles of Political Economy*, 1848.
[2]*Government and Industry*, P.E.P., 1952, p.1.

clingers-on to the classic theory found themselves forced to give ideological ground by the course of economic events.

Of course, there has never been total freedom from a government presence in the business of extracting resources and transforming them into finished goods. Taxes have been levied from earliest times, and the growth of the modern Budget has been attended by fiscal regulation of the "open market".

The dictum of free enterprise without any form of supervision or interference grew up in the years after the writings of Jeremy Bentham and his followers, and perhaps owed its origin as a business philosophy to Adam Smith, author of *The Wealth of Nations*. These early nineteenth-century radicals favoured the free operation of market forces, in which each manufacturer would compete with his neighbour, thus allowing the most efficient to emerge as the most profitable—and therefore the most socially beneficial. It is not hard to see why this view was attractive to the thrusting businessmen of the industrial revolution. It conferred on them what was virtually a divine right to grow and prosper.

But it rapidly became clear that, left to their own devices, this new aristocracy of industry might think only of the market forces, and not of the creatures so necessary to production. The appalling working conditions in the factories, and the growth of the trade unions, considered in Chapter 2, brought home to the governments of the day the fact that they had a responsibility to the working-classes. A massive body of legislation was passed, largely concerned with improving the conditions of workers in the factories, but, because the direction of pressure on government varied, there were also a number of Acts which strengthened the position of owners and employers in industry.

The first step towards the prevention of injury and the protection of labour in factories was taken in the Health and Morals of Apprentices Act of 1802, which put a stop to night work for apprentices and limited their hours of work to twelve. This Act also marked the beginning of the connection between factory legislation and the development of public education, for it contained clauses stipulating the kind of education to be given to apprentices. Further legislation followed in 1819, prohibiting child labour in the cotton industry under nine years of age and reinforcing the twelve-hour day, but it was not until the Factory Act of 1833 that legislation of this sort became effective. The 1833 Act introduced, for the first time, a Factory Inspectorate (with an initial strength of four) with the power to inspect and prosecute for breaches of the provisions on the employment of children.

The 1840s saw the beginning of government intervention in one of the country's major industries. The scandalous revelations of the Report of the Royal Commission on Labour in Mines and Manufactures in 1841—conditions so appalling as to have become almost legendary—led to the Mines Act of 1842. Further legislation regulating safety was passed in 1855, and in 1872 the Coal Mines Act attempted to provide a complete code of conduct for coal mines where there were special dangers to health, life and limb.

Another important breakthrough came in 1897 with the Workmen's Compensation Act, which introduced the principle that workers injured in accidents arising out of and in the course of their employment were entitled to be compensated by their employers.

None of these improvements in working conditions came easily. They all had to be fought for; governments only recognised their responsibility to the working people under extreme pressure from dedicated men like Robert Owen, who campaigned and organized for improvements, just as they campaigned and organized for the trade union movement. Legislation to deal with abuses often met great opposition and took years to put into effect. Even then it was never more than partially effective, and no attempt was made to meet the needs of industry as a whole.

The same period saw the beginnings of legislation in two other fields. Industrial education can be said to have begun with the 1802 Health and Morals of Apprentices Act, but it became a reality in 1837 with the founding of a Government School of Design. This was a school for apprentices which offered classes in the evenings, with both theoretical and practical instruction on textile design and manufacture. It seems to have been far in advance of its time, for the movement for industrial education did not really get going until the 1920s.

At the same time that the battle for the rights of workpeople to combine in trade unions was being fought, the employers were campaigning for the right to organize themselves in companies. The trend—already considered elsewhere—for businesses to become larger was hampered by the cumbersome machinery for forming a company—a necessary step if the risks of an enterprise were to be spread and limited. The Companies Clauses Consolidation Act of 1845, legislated on the constitution and management of joint stock companies. This Act was strengthened by the Companies Act of 1862, which made the formation of a company still easier by enacting that, provided that the object was lawful, any seven men could become a company with limited or unlimited liability merely by subscribing to a memorandum of association.

Other legislation affecting industry in this period related to land improvement, weights and measures, and public analysis. By the third quarter of the century, the cumulative effect of all this legislation was to change, albeit slowly, the philosophical base of Victorian industry. *Laissez-faire* could no longer be said to be the order of the day.

The Economist in 1894 exaggerated the speed of this change; "the state had assumed the character of a universal intervener"; in fact government intervention was limited to creating the right conditions for trade—not actually promoting trade on its own initiative.

The franchise extension and the reform of local government at the close of the century provided the springboard for a further, and unexpected, incursion by the public authorities into the private enterprise arena. Municipal trading, particularly in the utilities, spread rapidly in the North of England, Wales and Scotland. Though contemptuously referred to as "gas and water socialism", the new initiative became a source of concern to businessmen, who mobilized their resources to kill the ambitious schemes contemplated in some cities for municipal coal-mining, bread and milk companies, and fire insurance.

The advent of the telephone, and the growth of the monopolistic National Telephone Company, highlighted the problems of state versus private enterprise, and gave an indication of the collisions of interest to follow. The Post Office, the local authorities, and the NTC were given government sanction to operate telephone services. The small companies were either squeezed out or bought out by the NTC; the local authorities never seriously entered the field, and it gradually developed into a fight between the one private company left, and the GPO. It was an uneven struggle, of course, and the whole system was nationalized in 1912 by a Liberal government, in one of the very first state takeovers of industry.

But though few industries had been threatened by actual state takeover, there were many amalgamations of companies, a tendency which would have been deplored by the *laissez-faire* purists.

As Grove points out: "Collectivism was well established by the end of the century. The individualism of an earlier epoch was giving way to corporate enterprise, and although in the manufacturing industry the family business was not a thing of the past, it was fast yielding to the limited company run by salaried managers and owned by a large number of absentee shareholders."[1]

His view is supplemented by Allen, who asserts that "up to the First World War, practice accorded with theory . . . the government left business to its own devices, subject to the discipline of the market".[2]

Thus the stage was set for the great upheaval. Industry had collectivized itself to a substantial degree, and was now subject to a body of commercial and factory law. Apart from some government loans to particular industries (like the low-interest grant to Cunard to build *Mauretania* and *Lusitania*, and the purchase of a controlling interest in the Anglo-Persian Oil

[1] J. W. Grove, *Government and Industry in Britain,* 1962, p.27.
[2] G. C. Allen, *op. cit.,* p.107.

Company, now BP), state intervention had been kept to an unavoidable minimum.

The First World War provided both the opportunity and the motive for government intervention on a hitherto-undreamt-of scale. The waging of total war necessitated the mobilization of resources and productive capacity. But just as the nation was slow to appreciate the magnitude of the hostilities, so was it slow in putting into operation a vigorous programme of intervention.

As the Director-General of Raw Materials disclosed after the war: "The requirements, both on our own behalf and for our allies, increased by leaps and bounds. To obtain any proportionate increase of supplies was a matter of immense difficulty, and it gradually became evident that the task could not be left to undirected private enterprise. It was not possible to allow private importers to enjoy the almost unlimited opportunities of profit which would have been open to them. Still less was it possible to permit the amount and character of the available supplies to depend on their judgement, when any failure to make adequate provision would have had the most fatal consequences. From the beginning of 1916 onwards the true character of the problem began to show itself."[1]

It is something of a tribute to the efficiency of the *ancien régime* of business that it was two years before the British leadership had to intervene in the national interest. But this crucial decision, once taken, put on a formal basis a pattern of intervention which had grown only haphazardly since the declaration of hostilities.

The railways, mines and vital munitions factories came under government control. The merchant navy became the responsibility of the Ministry of Shipping. A Cotton Control Board took over the supply of materials to the industry, and a Directorate of Raw Materials was finally established in the summer of 1917. Food rationing was introduced, income tax went up to 6s. in the pound, and a large part of industrial profits went to the Exchequer.

[1]Ministry of Munitions, Raw Materials (Cmnd. 788, 1920) p.5.

One of the important factors of the World War One controls was that they were administered by senior managerial staff from the industries they controlled. This radical departure from Civil Service custom resulted in the growth of a new class of professionals: managers who knew both government and industry from the inside. And vice-versa, the government officials learned much from the industrial representatives.

Henceforth, whether the government withdrew from the industrial arena or not, there would still be a body of knowledge and experience which could be drawn upon in time of crisis.

In fact, at the end of the war, the emergency powers were revoked, the controls gradually abolished, and the consultative machinery was allowed to wither away. By the end of 1919, industry was in a position to operate much as it had before the war. But as the war poets reminded the public, nothing would be the same again.

Allen comments: "It is clear that government intervention in economic life, though still piecemeal rather than systematic, made a considerable advance between 1914 and the end of the first post-war decade. In the late 1920s the ratio of government expenditure (central government, local authorities, and payments from social insurance funds) to the gross national product was more than twice that before the war, and the state's activities had grown not only by development along lines familiar before 1914 but by extension in new directions. Yet the system of private enterprise had undergone no fundamental modification."[1]

But, after the war, industry showed little signs of returning to the relatively high production levels achieved before it. The introduction of the McKenna duties on imported goods was justified as an emergency measure to save valuable shipping space and foreign exchange. But they were kept on after the war was over, and further tariff laws were brought in during the 1920s, culminating in the blanket Import Duties Act of 1932, which signified the final flight from free trade into protectionism. This Act provided for a ten per cent tax on all foreign goods except certain Empire produce. These taxes were extended in the

[1] G. C. Allen, *op. cit.* p.109.

years leading up to the Second War, and import quotas were also introduced.

The economic conditions surrounding this historic withdrawal from the trading policy which had been the foundation of Britain's pre-eminence throughout the period of the industrial revolution and afterwards were those of slump, affecting both this country's industry and that of the world. Legislation was passed to protect home industry, to reduce unemployment, and later to encourage firms to site new productive capacity in areas where the staple industries were rapidly declining.

Scarcity of manpower and resources for industry during the war had already led to the establishment of committees to examine specific industrial problems (the precedent for such committees and commissions went back to the nineteenth century, when agricultural depression and industrial depression were, respectively, examined by Royal Commissions). The Whitley Committee was set up during the First World War "to make and consider suggestions for securing a permanent improvement in the relations between employers and workmen, and to recommend means for securing that industrial conditions affecting the relations between employers and workmen shall be systematically reviewed by those concerned, with a view to improving conditions in the future." The Committee reported in 1917 and 1918 and recommended that Joint Industrial Councils should be set up with the object of establishing closer co-operation between employers and employees. These were to include representatives of the Ministry of Labour, who would act in an advisory capacity. The Committee also advocated the setting up of Trade Boards to be specifically linked with the Industrial Councils, thus expanding the original purpose of Trade Boards, which was the setting of minimum wages. The Committee stated, however, that "we do not . . . regard Government assistance as an alternative to the organization of employers and employed". The Committee also made the important recommendation that governments wishing to consult with industries should do so through the medium of the Joint Industrial Councils and not through the Trade Boards. In 1924 the Whitley Committee suggestions were put into effect by the Joint Industrial Councils Act. The idea of a National Industrial Council, however, was still being discussed by the Committee on Industry and Trade in 1929. This Committee was created during the depression to consider such matters as unemployment, wage rates and the like. In times of depression even industrialists are prone to welcome government intervention which, in times of prosperity, they reject as interference.

The period between the wars also saw the beginning of government intervention in the rationalization of industry. It was necessary to restructure the country's productive capacity, and the government set about this by use of long-term loans, guarantees and subsidies. A list of the industries involved reads like an inventory of the nation's resources : it included coal, cotton, shipbuilding, shipping, road haulage and road passenger transport, agriculture, steel and civil aviation. There were many examples of government generosity towards individual firms who found themselves unable to raise capital for major projects through the usual channels. Ten million pounds were loaned through the Bank of England to Richard Thomas's Ebbw Vale steelworks in 1935; Cunard were given a loan to complete the *Queen Mary* and to build the *Queen Elizabeth*.

This continuing process led to strong demands for a General Enabling Act which would give the government powers to promote rationalization in any industry which felt in need of it. Several bills on these lines were debated in Parliament, but both sides of industry opposed the introduction of such an Act for vested reasons of their own. Businessmen disliked it on principle, and trade unionists wanted full public ownership without half-measures.

The economist, J. M. Keynes, whose ideas were later to exert a profound influence on Labour politicians, counselled the government of the day to intervene in order to exercise a guiding influence on private industry. His advice was in effect carried out, but it was through the pressure of economic circumstances, rather than the weight of intellectual argument. As the slump was world-wide, so was the trend to intervene, especially in the United States.

The view of *The Economist*, given in early 1939, is worth quoting in full to recall the dramatic change in thinking which the country had undergone between the wars: "Until the last decade or so it was the accepted doctrine among virtually all businessmen and perhaps more than half the public that the state would intervene in the affairs of specific industries as little as possible. Complete *laissez-faire* went by the board decades ago, but until recently the tendency has been, at least among businessmen, to regard state intervention as perhaps necessary, but if so a necessary evil. As a purely abstract proposition that would still doubtless be maintained.

"But in practice the attitude has changed. The change dates from the Great Depression and from its economic consequence in Great Britain, the protective tariff. Since 1932 the state has no longer appeared to industry solely in the guise of monitor or policeman; it has favours to dispense.

"What is more, in addition to the concealed subsidy of a Customs duty, the state has begun to hand out specific subsidies in hard cash, from which agriculture has benefited most handsomely, but by no means exclusively. And finally, in addition to tariff protection and cash subsidies, the state has in several cases lent its aid to the creation of legally enforceable determinations of minimum price and maximum output. The result has naturally been to revolutionize the attitude of industry to the state: the policeman has turned Father Christmas."[1]

A similar view had been expressed some four years before by the moderate "Next Five Years Group", which said in a manifesto: "We believe that the state will find it increasingly necessary to intervene, in order to set the direction of the economic activity of the community. The old self-regulating mechanism of a competitive economy, guided by the prospect of profits, is not by itself an adequate regulator of the whole system. . . . The nation will rightly require of its government not merely a passive policy of succouring the victims of a defective economy,

[1]*The Economist*, 18 March 1939, p.551.

but a positive, energetic leadership in constructing a new organization for collective planning and direction of economic life."[1]

One of the signatories to this manifesto was Harold Macmillan, who as a Prime Minister of the 1960s was to preside over a return to state intervention by a Conservative administration.

The 1929 Committee on Industry and Trade referred to above also made important recommendations in two other fields affecting the relationship of government and industry: technical education and research sponsorship.

There were reports on the relationship between public education, technical education, and the requirements of trade and industry in 1925 and 1927, but it was the Report of the Committee on Trade and Industry in 1929 which finally recognized "education as a factor in industrial and commercial efficiency". The Committee was concerned with the training of boys and girls on a regular basis to fill vacancies in industrial establishments. It emphasized the need to train young people for particular industrial skills and to do this within the system of state education. The Committee thought that each industry should analyse its needs and report them to the educational authority, and suggested possible machinery for ensuring appropriate training, including the establishment of a Department of State, inter-departmental co-operation, or an *ad hoc* National Committee. It advised that teaching in technical and art schools should be on a more practical basis and that the teaching staff should be required to "devote a sufficient amount of time to research or to the actual practice of a craft". Such advice on the adjustment of the education system to meet industrial needs is more than ever applicable and pertinent today, when there is increasing emphasis on the possession of technical skills, and a corresponding extension of facilities for technical and higher technological education.

As with education, so with technology—or the application of science to industry. Government interest in this area began

[1] *The Next Five Years: An Essay in Political Agreement*, 1935, pp. 12-13.

in 1900 with the setting up of the National Physical Laboratory, and continued with the establishment of the Development Commission in 1909, the Medical Research Committee in 1913, and the department of government which later became the Department of Scientific and Industrial Research, in 1915. This Department, whose function was to develop and organize the knowledge required for the application of science to industry, was to keep in close touch with all Departments concerned with scientific research, to undertake research on behalf of Departments and stimulate the supply of research workers.

But it was once again the Committee on Industry and Trade which emphasized the need for industry to recognize the value of scientific research, and pointed out the difference in the US and Germany, where "a very great amount of research has been carried out by industrial associations, corporations, combinations, and even by large industrial concerns". The Committee recognized the need for "strategical" research—the search for new processes—rather than "tactical" research—the improvement of results from known processes. They suggested that the research associations should communicate their results to industry in language that could be understood by industrialists, and suggested that industry should employ personnel specially trained to "receive" the findings of the scientists and "interpret" them to industry. The Committee also emphasized the need for state financial aid from the Department of Scientific and Industrial Research if technological research were to advance at the required pace.

And so, by the 1930s, economic necessity had driven government and industry together in ways that would not have been thought possible before the First World War, and the foundations of twentieth-century industrialism had been laid. Industry had become too important to the nation's health for it to be possible for any government to allow it to sink or swim according to the forces of the market—industry's survival meant Britain's survival. When the 1939–45 war broke out, both the lessons learned from the previous war and contingency planning were put into action. Government controls were introduced immediately, and taxation and licensing measures were brought into operation. The government allocated raw materials on a priority basis, and certain consumer goods were selected to bear a prohibitive rate of purchase tax.

The Control Staffs were headed by leaders of the respective industries, and, building on the experience of the previous war, trade associations were widely used to allocate raw materials and determine pricing policy. There was a large measure of co-operation between industrialists and the wartime government.

As Grove points out, the war changed the relationship between the government and industry in three major respects. First, it gave rise to a tradition of close co-operation between organized industry (management, labour and technology) and the central administration. Secondly, the government accepted—for the first time—responsibility for economic planning, manifested in the 1944 White Paper on Employment Policy after the war. Thirdly, each Ministry took on the job of sponsoring certain sectors of industry, which during the war meant managing its controls and resources, and afterwards gave the Ministry a "caretaker" role for the sponsored industries.[1]

When the war ended, there was not the same rush to abandon controls as there had been in 1918. Acute shortages of all raw materials, bombed factories, and the problems of demobilization of armed services scattered over the four points of the earth made a simple return to pre-war conditions impossible. And the people did not want it. The climate of opinion had swung in favour of planning. The election of 1945 was a landslide for Labour, who rightly or wrongly interpreted it as a sign that the electorate was in favour of a planned growth economy, and set about building one.

The government did not sell back any of the undertakings taken into the public sector during the war, and added several more before losing office in 1951. Thus between 1939 and 1951, the railways, together with their hotel, shipping and other interests, road haulage, electricity supply, gas supply, coal, aviation, iron and steel, raw cotton marketing and the Bank

[1] J. W. Grove, op. cit., p.61.

of England had either been nationalized or were the subject of legislation to make them State owned.

Although the idea of nationalization can be said to have been an article of faith in the socialism of the 1940s, this was not the only reason why those industries which were nationalized were selected. This is no place for a detailed history of the factors leading to nationalization, but a consideration of the general pattern illustrates once again that government intervention was dictated by events rather than theory. In the case of each public service industry which became nationalized the concern of the government was initially stimulated by a failure on either a local or regional level of the supply of services to meet public demand.

This failure was responsible for the railways being made subject to some degree of state control as far back as 1840, and for the regulation of the gas industry in 1847, and for the Macmillan Committee Report on the Bank of England in 1930. The form which nationalization took varied from industry to industry, as did the control exercised by the Minister responsible. An excellent summary of this role was given by Lord Justice (now Lord) Denning in the case of *Tamlin v. Hannaford* :

"The protection of the interests of . . . the taxpayer, user and beneficiary, is entrusted by Parliament to the Minister. . . . He is given powers . . . which are as great as those possessed by a man who holds all the shares in a private company, subject, however, as such a man is not, to a duty to account to Parliament for his stewardship . . . he is given powers to give them directions of a general nature, in matters which appear to him to affect the national interest, as to which he is the sole judge, and they [the directors] are then bound to obey."[1]

Nationalization apart, one of the first acts of the Labour government was to initiate a survey of the economy. This document was not on the lines of the French "Plans" : it did not lay down detailed objectives for each industry but gave forecasts (interpreted as government targets) which it hoped to see achieved at the end of the year. As a public relations exercise,

[1][1950] 1 K.B.18 at p.23.

the plan was a huge success; 440,000 copies of the popular version were sold. Later years saw the publication of further surveys, couched in less definitive language.

Labour's planning has been criticized by the economist Andrew Shonfield as showing ignorance of long-term needs. His verdict was :

"Certainly it [the government] allowed itself to be disappointed too easily when it discovered that its initial facile vision of limitless possibilities for the application of frictionless controls did not correspond with the facts of economic or political life. But it never seems to have made any effort to adjust the techniques to these facts. The truth is that the whole operation of Labour planning, when it worked at all, was directed to strictly short-term objectives."[1]

One of Labour's most significant experiments was the setting up of working parties in seventeen industries under Board of Trade auspices, which recommended the establishment of Development Councils in eleven of them. These were duly authorized by the 1947 Industrial Organization and Development Act. But the Act specified that the councils had to be "desired by a substantial number of persons engaged in the industry". Some of the wartime co-operative spirit had by this time evaporated. Only four were actually set up, two of which were boycotted by the industry they were designed to restructure.

The Labour administration, which had kept controls on finance, commerce, raw materials and company investment and profits, began to slacken the economic reins towards the end of its tenure of office, with a series of "bonfires" of controls.

But the nation's mood swung again in 1951, when there was a substantial body of opinion in the Tory party which wanted a return to unfettered free enterprise, which in the nostalgic minds of some, existed just before the war, but which in fact disappeared after 1914. When the Conservatives were returned to power, steel was given back to the former private owners, who had put up a fierce struggle to stop nationalization going

[1]Andrew Shonfield, *Modern Capitalism*, 1965, p. 89.

through. Road haulage was denationalized, and so was raw-cotton marketing. The majority of financial and raw material controls were dismantled, and the rest was left as before. The welfare state and basic nationalized industries were intact, and for a decade, the Conservative government was content to administer an apparatus inherited from Labour.

It was in the early 1960s that another change of mood began to make itself felt. The joint industry-trade-government National Economic Development Council was set up in 1962 with the object of achieving more effective ways of co-ordinating economic policy. Its terms of reference were :

(a) to examine the economic performance of the nation with particular concern for plans for the future in both the public and private sectors of industry;

(b) to consider together what are the obstacles to quicker growth, what can be done to improve efficiency, and whether the best use is being made of our resources; and

(c) to seek agreement upon ways of improving economic performance, competitive power and efficiency, in other words, to increase the rate of sound growth.

The Council is made up of representatives of Government, Management and the Trade Unions. It is outside the machinery of government and is independent of the Treasury. It is in effect a parliament of economic interest groups. Its members are responsible to the organizations which nominate them, and present their cases for particular policies and specific priorities accordingly. No action can be taken on any recommendation unless agreement is achieved by the members.

The same year, 1962, saw the reorganization of the Treasury and, inside the Ministry, the establishment of an economy group, a finance group, and a public sector group, so that the department had almost an echo of Stafford Cripps's organization. These reforms, carried out under the Premiership of Harold Macmillan, marked a move to a more sophisticated style of government intervention : the doctrine of the "hidden hand".

A further impetus towards planning was Britain's application to join the European Economic Community, which required, in Shonfield's words, "a far-ranging review" of the economy as a basis for argument with members of the Six. Unhappily, the de Gaulle veto stifled this promising project before it had properly got off the ground. One of the casualties of rejection was the dismemberment of the Cabinet sub-committee chaired by R. A. Butler, then First Secretary of State, which was examining the economy. This committee's work, and the general process it represented, comments Shonfield : "supplied an impulse towards administrative reform *inside* the government, which did not altogether lose its momentum. Summing up the process as it appeared at the election in 1964, it may be said that the intellectual and administrative preconditions for modern capitalist planning had been created or were in course of being established. This represented a remarkable change of attitude on the Right of British politics."[1]

Possibly this was only another aspect of the technological consciousness which was developing and whose essence was so ably caught by Harold Wilson at Scarborough in 1964. Certainly, the Labour government's movement towards further involvement with industry through the creation of the Ministry of Technology was in line with national as well as socialist thinking. A further dimension was added to the relationship of government and industry with the creation in 1966 of the Industrial Reorganization Corporation, whose purpose is the promotion and assistance for reorganization or development in any industry and, at the request of the Secretary of State, the establishment, promotion, development or assistance of any industrial enterprise—a valuable aid to the necessary restructuring of industry.

Conclusions

If the various roles that governments have played in their relationships with industry over the last 150 years are examined, it will be seen that their degree of involvement at any particular time is the inevitable result of their historical situation. Political

[1]A. Shonfield, *op. cit.*, pp. 108-9.

theory may contribute to the solution of a given problem, but the needs of industry itself and of society generally play the major part. Governments are pragmatic—circumstances usually prevent them from being anything else.

In the case of the trade union movement and of factory legislation the government found itself legislating as arbitrator between the demands of the employers and the needs of the workers. Government's role was that of arbiter of social justice—and this is a role which governments still play today in their relationship with industry. Its most recent manifestations have been in such Acts as the Redundancy Payments Act, 1965, and the Contracts of Employment Act, 1963, which have brought greater security to the employee.

In times of emergency, war and economic depression, the government's role was a controlling one, aimed at husbanding the nation's resources and using them with the utmost efficiency—the methods varied, sometimes direct control was necessary, sometimes an advisory role was sufficient. The lessons learned during these periods of crisis have been taken to heart, and government's role has extended to one of sponsorship and investment for the future.

Government can thus be said to have a three-fold responsibility in its involvement with industry. First, in the provision of jobs, and the maintenance of the flow of work both nationally and regionally; secondly, in the provision of services, e.g., fuel, transport, communications; thirdly, in the management of the nation's resources.

It is this third area which remains controversial; for, while it seems to be generally agreed that it is the responsibility of the government to develop both natural and industrial resources in terms of the present and future needs of the nation, there is still one sector of the Conservative Party, lately become vocal in the person of Sir Keith Joseph, which thinks that the development of industry is best left to industry itself.

It is my purpose to show that this philosophy is wrong. Not only is it necessary for government to be actively involved in industrial affairs in the nation's interest, but industry must recognize that it needs the help government can give. To argue otherwise is to put the clock back—not merely ten years, but fifty. But neither party to the partnership is fully equipped to work together efficiently and in the following chapters I shall endeavour to show not only why industry needs government interest and involvement, but how both government and industry can become more efficient.

5

INDUSTRIES OF INNOVATION:

THREE CASE STUDIES

THE REASONS WHY governments, of whatever political colour, have felt it necessary to involve themselves with industry, are clearly demonstrated by the history of their relations. The question which remains to be answered is "Why does industry need the help of government?" The answer has already been touched on in the previous chapter : since the early 1930s the role of the state is not only one of controlling or restraining industry; the state now has favours to dispense.

And industry needs these favours : to argue, as Sir Keith Joseph and other spokesmen do, that ninety-five per cent of British industry needs no special help from the government, seems to show a poor understanding of what the needs of industry are. The functions of government and industry are, as he points out, very different. Of course, the objectives of companies are precise, defined, objectives—relating to their primary function of profit-making—and those of government much more general, because industry is only part of the complex society they are concerned with, but the roles of the two are not mutually exclusive, and in some areas, if the two do not work together, offering mutual aid and support, industrial and national disaster could follow. We may not be facing a threat of the dimensions of the two great wars or the depression of the thirties, but we are everywhere facing a challenge : a challenge to our industries and their ability to lead or keep up with their competitors in international markets.

This challenge comes primarily from the United States. Despite the enormous contribution British inventions have made to modern industrial knowledge, as a result of our failure to adapt this knowledge to industrial use and to keep up with the pace of change at production as well as laboratory level, the United States and the Soviet Union now hold pre-eminent places in the world markets. So far as Western Europe is concerned, and that includes Britain, it means that the United States is a competitor not only in world markets but on our own doorstep, controlling large sectors of key industries.

The main reason why we have been able to keep up with the American advance, even to a limited extent, is because the pressures of the Second World War brought industry, science and government into a working relationship, and we have consistently advanced targets and budgets in research and development until we are now spending, taking both public and private sectors, close on £1,000 million annually—two-thirds of the total amount for the whole of Europe.

But scientific and technological advance is becoming increasingly complex, uncertain and expensive. No company whose function it is to make profits can afford the risk of investigating a blind alley; failure is too expensive. But the cost of ignoring new developments can be equally great, involving a steady loss of markets to competitors, and eventual decline. It is at this point that industry must be able to turn to the state and ask for help in pursuing a new process; and it is for the state to arm itself so that it can evaluate such requests, investigate and finance investigation of new techniques and inventions; and assist them to commercial viability. The role of sponsor is probably the most important of all government's roles in its relationship with industry.

The research which the government does on its own behalf also has commercial applications, and it is the business of government to see that, where these exist, they are fully exploited by industry. The main area of government research in the past has been in the field of defence, which has involved the government in the sponsorship of research laboratories, armaments manufacture, and the building of particular types of equipment. There is an inevitable "spin-off" in the form of devices and techniques which are applicable to purposes other than those for which they were developed. This is sometimes small, but it is nevertheless an important way in which the benefits of research are passed on to private industry and sometimes to the community at large.

A good example of government involvement of this sort is the Ministry of Defence's chemical and biological research establishment at Porton Down in Wiltshire. There are, naturally, ethical and emotional issues involved in the particular work carried out at the Chemical Defence Establishment and the Microbiological Research Establishment, but there is no doubt that the knowledge gained in the pursuit of so-called defence has constructive uses which affect private industry, primarily the pharmaceutical industry. The two establishments have developed techniques of bacterial cultivation which have helped in the manufacture of vaccines and antibiotics. They have also developed air filtration units for installation in buildings and ships, and an alarm system which gives instantaneous warning of the presence of nerve gases. There is also a productive relationship between the government research establishments and the universities. It was recently reported that there are twenty-seven research contracts arranged between Porton and the universities.

Defence has also provided opportunity for the government to exercise its sponsorship, as well as its research, function but, as the aircraft industry has found to its cost, dependence on satisfying military needs is not enough to ensure prosperity. This industry is heavily dependent on overseas markets; the cost of developing a new type of aeroplane is so enormous that only by being first in the field can any aircraft manufacturer expect to cover his development costs; and in the past twenty years or so, innovation in the aircraft industry has been so rapid that, unless there has been a speedy advance from conception to production, some aircraft have been obsolete before the first one has flown.

It is, indeed, innovation that makes modern industry so dependent on government sponsorship. The realization of the

importance of innovation was, as the last chapter has demonstrated, first fully appreciated by the government in 1929, when
the Committee on Industry and Technology emphasized the
need for continuous state financial aid to the work of the Department of Scientific and Industrial Research. A further step in
the right direction was taken in 1948 with the setting up of the
National Research Development Corporation. This is a public
corporation with members drawn from science, industry and the
world of finance, appointed by the Minister of Technology. Its
function is the formation of a link between research and industry,
assisting the flow of new ideas and techniques into industry,
with the object of obtaining a due return for the money spent in
creating and developing such techniques. It directs the commercial exploitation of patent rights in inventions derived from
publicly-supported research and also underwrites the development of promising inventions which seem to be in the national
interest.

One aspect of the Corporation's work is the joint ventures with
industry in which, for example, an industrial firm invites the
NRDC to share with it the cost of developing a new invention
or process. This is usually a project which the company has
already started but which it is unwilling to continue because of
the high risk, or because it cannot be supported on an adequate
scale from the company's own resources. NRDC can also help
in the application of known processes in new environments or
with the introduction of new machines or technology. The
most expensive and one of the most successful projects the
Corporation has undertaken to date is the development of the
hovercraft, the invention of a private individual.

Some 80 per cent of NRDC's work comes from outside its
laboratories, since it functions principally by financing research
elsewhere. In addition, the government spends some £180
million per year on research in its own laboratories; the work
is spread over a number of different agencies and organizations;
among the best known are the Atomic Energy Authority, the
National Physical Laboratory, and the Royal Radar and Royal
Aircraft Establishments. The future of these institutions and

of the NRDC, including their future relationship with industry, is, at present, under review by the government.[1] What that future should be is discussed below; how the government/ industry partnership works at present in industries of innovation is illustrated by the following three case studies.

CASE STUDIES

The Nuclear Power Industry

From the beginning, the government had an interest in the nuclear power industry. The early history of the industry is tied up with general nuclear research which, because of its defence aspects, was largely government controlled.

By the early 1950s, however, it was realized that nuclear power could be developed as an economic source of electricity. A reactor design team was brought together by the Atomic Energy Board, which was then under the control of the Ministry of Supply. The team's first task was the designing of the Windscale reactor, a research project, and they then went on to design Calder Hall, the first operational power station reactor. By 1954 a civil atomic energy policy had been formulated, the basic aims of which were: to secure the general development of the new technology as rapidly as possible; to seek to meet the requirements of the generating authorities; and to develop and exploit export markets for British reactors and fuels.

To this end the United Kingdom Atomic Energy Authority was set up under the Atomic Energy Act, 1954. The principal function of the Authority has been research and development, and successive Ministers on whom responsibility for atomic energy has fallen have relied extensively on the advice of the Authority as to the priority to be accorded to different elements in the programme, and all questions of technical and economic assessment, as well as the day-to-day running of the Authority have been left to the Chairman of the Authority and his Board.

[1]*Industrial Research and Development in Government Laboratories,* HMSO, 1970.

The building of the first nuclear power stations presented many practical difficulties in that there was an almost total absence of operating or commercial experience in this field. In addition, the building of so large and problematical an undertaking as a nuclear generating station involved considerable financial risk; the government therefore invited firms having appropriate specialist capacities in, for example, boiler making, turbine construction, large-scale concrete construction, and the like, to join together to take on "turnkey" contracts. From these initial arrangements grew the consortia of companies specialising in nuclear power stations.

In 1958 the Central Electricity Generating Board assumed overall responsibility for the supply of electricity in England and Wales, within the framework of the national fuel policy as laid down by the Ministry of Power. By 1967 they had nine nuclear power stations operational, including the two originating with the Atomic Energy Authority and four more under construction. The CEGB operated by keeping the consortia informed of their future plant requirements; at the appropriate stage the consortia, originally five but by 1967 reduced to three, tender for the complete power station.

In 1966 twenty-five British designed power reactors accounted for 63 per cent of the world's installed nuclear generating capacity. Nevertheless, it could not be said that the industry commanded the world market so far as exports of reactors were concerned, for the only contracts outside of Britain were for two relatively small stations, one in Italy and one in Japan, obtained before there was any serious competition from America. The development by America of two water reactors with which the British reactor could not compete led to a withdrawal from the export market until 1966, when the British Nuclear Export Executive, a partnership of the consortia and the Atomic Energy Authority, was formed to promote sales of British reactors.

This was the situation so far as the structure and functions of the industry were concerned in 1966–67 when the House of Commons Select Committee on Science and Technology, of which I was a member, investigated and reported on the nuclear power industry.[1] In that Report the Committee made various recommendations designed to make the industry more efficient at home and more competitive abroad. We recommended that the consortium system of tendering for contracts should be phased out and that the generating boards should be free to place orders for nuclear stations on the same basis as they do for other types of power station; that the AEA's function should be limited to pure research and development; that the best interests of the country would be served by the combination in a single organization or company of the skill and resources of those now separately engaged in the design and construction of nuclear boilers; and that the British Nuclear Export Executive be wound up and a potential survey of potential overseas needs in this field be put in hand at once by the Board of Trade. We also made recommendations as to the development of the different types of reactor considered below, as well as on the development of nuclear power for other purposes.

In 1968, the Minister of Technology, under whose authority the Atomic Energy Authority had fallen on the creation of that Ministry, made a statement in the House of Commons[2] in which he referred to the consultations conducted by the Industrial Reorganization Corporation, as a result of which he had written formally to the Chairman of the Corporation inviting his assistance "in the creation of *two* design and construction organizations to be established in place of the three commercial firms and design teams working within the Atomic Energy Authority" (italics mine). When in April 1969 the Select Committee began to take evidence for a follow-up report the process of reorganization had so far produced two companies substantially the same as two of the previously existing consortia, the only new feature being the substantial shareholding in the new companies of the Atomic Energy Authority (20 per cent in each) and of the Industrial Reorganization Corporation (26 per cent in one and 10 per cent in the other). The third consortium is still in existence on paper only, its demise being delayed by

[1]H.C. 381 (1966–67).
[2]*Hansard*, 17 July 1968, Col. 1428.

difficulties in the construction of Dungeness "B" power station.

The Committee concluded in its second Report on the industry[1] that in spite of all the time and energy that have been devoted to the reorganization of the industry, very little has been achieved so far to rationalize, strengthen and make it more competitive in world markets.

There are, at present, three types of reactors currently attracting the interests of overseas customers. These are the Mark II gas cooled reactor, the Steam Generating Heavy Water Reactor and the High Temperature Reactor.

The Advanced Gas-Cooled Reactor has been ordered by the Central Electricity Generating Board and by the South of Scotland Electricity Board for four power stations for which contracts have recently been placed. One company, The Nuclear Power Group Limited, considers this type of reactor to be up-to-date and to have export potential, although it would need to become significantly, rather than marginally, more attractive before customers used to the techniques of water reactor operating could be induced to transfer their interest to it.

The second type of reactor is the Steam Generating Heavy Water Reactor. At present neither of the new companies is licensed to sell it, licences having been withheld by the Minister pending the reorganization of the industry. The Atomic Energy Authority consider this type of reactor as promising, especially in units of 400MW and below, and as safe, and thus suitable for siting in populated areas. British Nuclear Design and Construction Limited are exploring potential markets in Finland, Greece, Argentina and New Zealand.

Finally, there is the High Temperature reactor based on the Dragon reactor at Winfrith, which has been operating successfully since August 1964. There are small prototype HTRs operating in the USA and Germany, and sufficient experience with the system has accumulated for demonstration reactors to be offered in both countries. This reactor has further advantages in that there is a potential improvement in the system which, it is estimated, could lead to a reduction of generation costs of

[1]H.S. 401 (1968–69).

5 to 6 per cent. The comparable German system is calculated by them to be likely to account for a greater proportion of installed capacity than fast reactors. It would make good sense if the plans for technical improvement be accepted and if a bilateral agreement between the German and British industrial firms interested in this development be encouraged.

The tendency in the major European countries has been to install water reactors purchased from the United States or built under licence. Our own manufacturers, meanwhile, have concentrated on gas reactors for the home market where the few possible purchasers have chosen up until now to use nothing else. The result is that British manufacturers have been getting steadily more expert in a branch of nuclear technology which has not proved attractive to potential buyers overseas. By comparison, the Winfrith reactor, which has functioned so superbly and which is an example to possible foreign customers of a water reactor which the British industry is capable of constructing, has been virtually ignored. No reactor of this type has yet been ordered for the commercial electricity supply network in this country and until this is done, foreign buyers are less likely to be convinced that a British-made water reactor should be bought by them. In these circumstances the industry must either show that the Advanced Gas-Cooled Reactor is significantly cheaper than its competitors or they must decide to give the High Temperature Reactor priority as the leading reactor for export.

Apart from the indecision over which reactor should be developed there is considerable lack of co-ordinated effort in selling British reactors abroad. It is probably very difficult for a foreign customer to be sure of the most effective way of obtaining information about British-made reactors. British engineering representatives abroad are probably not representing the nuclear consortia as such, but are more likely to be members of the firms making up the consortia: if this is the case, their knowledge of nuclear matters and enthusiasm for reactor sales may not be as informed as could be desired. Alternatively, a customer may already be aware of the Atomic Energy Authority's expertise and past activities in his country and may decide to make his approach direct to the Authority. He may decide to approach the British Embassy, and, despite the confidence shown in them by the companies, the commercial departments of United Kingdom missions abroad are not very clear who in Britain is responsible for handling export inquiries. It is essential to the future of the industry that this uncertainty as to whom to approach be cleared up. There is a growing independent German effort in the manufacture of economical reactors which will make the international market even more competitive in the near future, and the British industry cannot afford such ambiguities.

The Select Committee made the valid point that had the intensive survey of potential overseas nuclear needs and opportunities which they recommended in the first Report been carried out, the three Departments concerned would have been able to launch an all-out drive in conjunction with the industry and with the financial backing of the Export Credits Guarantee Department to secure world-wide interest in British nuclear exports. This opportunity has been missed.

There is confusion, also, in the lines of demarcation between the work of the Atomic Energy Authority and the work of the companies. The Committee's view is that the Atomic Energy Board which it is proposed should be set up to formalise collaboration in the expensive field of fundamental research and its commercial deployment is a matter of great urgency if research, development, manufacture, application and sales are to be more appropriately linked together. It is no good resting on our laurels—the triumphs of the 1950s: these must be regarded as incidents in an honourable past and present reality must become the spur to success in the harsher economic climate of the 1970s.

The future may not, however, be as gloomy as the Select Committee's Report forecasts. The German chemical industry has shown an interest in the Advanced Gas-Cooled Reactor: in industries such as these, requiring superheated steam as well as electricity, price is not the first consideration, and it is reasonable to be optimistic about sales in this area in the near future. Such new markets cannot, however, be taken for granted—the industry must go out and seek them.

The Computer Industry

At the end of the Second World War, two companies in England, Ferranti Ltd. and Lyons, sent representatives to the United States to learn where the most advanced computer work was being carried out. To their surprise they were both told it was being done in England. As a result, Ferranti Ltd. began to work with Professor Williams at Manchester University and Lyons with Dr. Wilkes at Cambridge.

Meanwhile, the two long-established British punched card companies had decided to break their links with their American parent-companies, an action supported by the British government, which was worried by the outflow of dollars. The move was also supported by the United States government, whose anti-trust legislation was aimed at reducing the control of such powerful companies over the world market. What the two British companies, British Tabulation Machines and Powers-Samas, did not fully appreciate at first was that they were cutting themselves off from research and development at a time when their market was radically changing as a result of the introduction of the computer. The result was that their businesses did not prosper as much as they had done in the past; they therefore decided that they should join forces in order to benefit from the economies of rationalization. This they did in 1959, forming International Computers and Tabulators Limited (ICT). They still had not resolved the question of research and development, however, and the merger was not, therefore, the unmitigated success which had been anticipated. When the message did, finally, get home, they decided to purchase research and development ability and in 1961 computer engineers and designers of the General Electric Company, Ltd., Great Britain, joined ICT; in July 1962 the Commercial Computer Division of EMI was added to the company and finally, in September

1963, the Commercial Computer Department of Ferranti Ltd. joined the ICT Group.

A parallel process of rationalization led to the formation of English Electric Computers Limited. In April 1963, the data processing and control systems division of English Electric and Leo Computers Limited came together as English Electric Leo Computers Limited. English Electric bought out Lyons' share of the company in October 1964 and at the same time, Marconi's commercial and scientific computer interests were added to the company which was then re-named English Electric-Leo-Marconi Computers Limited. In March 1967 the name changed again to English Electric Computers, and in August of the same year Elliott Automation Computers was added to the group when Elliott Automation merged with English Electric.

In 1964 ICT introduced the first British computer to be truly commercially successful, the 1900 Series. With this series they knew that they could challenge the American domination of the world computer market. Their confidence was not shared by all in the outside world, particularly not in political circles. One senior Tory leader was reported to have remarked that "the sooner the British computer industry sank beneath the waves and allowed the Americans to get on with the job, the better". Naturally enough, ICT disagreed, believing that it would be a serious error of strategy to allow the country's computer requirements to be supplied entirely from abroad. Their own experience had shown them that the computer was to become the focal point of all successful, large organizations and that foreign control of such an important area of the economy could have serious political disadvantages. This point of view was put forward by the directors of the Company but they found that this activity, so essential to their survival, was taking up too much of their time. They decided, therefore, to appoint a full time Government Relations Officer whose task it would be to work for the formation of a viable, indigenous British computer industry.

Prior to the 1964 election, the Labour Party realized that science and technology, hitherto subjects of little political appeal, had become both fashionable and a matter of genuine concern to the growing number of young technocrats throughout the country. This rationalization was reflected in Harold Wilson's Scarborough speech and ICT decided to take full advantage of this development in political thinking. A document was prepared with considerable care by the Company which dealt in detail with the future relationship required between the British computer industry and Her Majesty's Government. This document was injected into every level of government and Parliament and when, on 1 March 1965, Mr. Frank Cousins, the first Minister of Technology, made a statement about the computer industry, the policy he laid down reflected strongly the policy expressed in ICT's document. Mr. Cousins said that "The government consider that it is essential that there should be a rapid increase in the use of computer and computer techniques in industry and commerce, and that there should be a flourishing British computer industry. Plans have been prepared to serve these ends."

The British computer industry took great care to work with the growing Ministry of Technology and excellent working relationships were built up from the Chairmen and the Minister downwards throughout the working levels of the Ministry and the industry. Probably for the first time, civil servants made an all-out effort to understand the workings of the industry that they were sponsoring and in the same way industry began to appreciate the pattern of behaviour that government administration imposes upon the Civil Service. As confidence between the two sides grew the degree of contact expanded and became a matter of everyday procedure. At no time did the close relationship between government and the industry develop to a point where the government could be said to be interfering with the day-to-day management of the Company.

However, design and production of modern computers requires increasingly large investments of money and manpower; the trend is thus towards larger firms. Because computers are so important in many fields of national activity, and are certain to become more and more important, a strong British computer industry organized on the right lines is needed to ensure that our main aims in this field are achieved. The most important step in this direction was taken in March 1968, after long discussion and with strong support from the Ministry, by the creation of International Computers Limited (ICL). ICL is the result of a merging of the commercial and scientific businesses of International Computers and Tabulators Limited and English Electric Computers. It is by far the largest company outside the USA specializing in these types of computers. Plessey, a major manufacturer of telecommunications equipment, has also participated in the new group.

In recognition of the need for ICL to undertake a large research and development programme the government, through the Ministry, is participating in the financing of the new company to the extent of £17 million over a period of five years. £13½ million of this money will be paid as grants towards ICL's research and development expenditure; the remaining £3½ million is to be subscribed for ordinary shares of £1 each, issued to the government at par. These terms have been designed to make a high proportion of the government's contribution available as support for the research and development programme chargeable against revenue, while giving the Government a substantial participation in the future prosperity of the Company which this programme is designed to secure.

Nor is government support for the industry limited to investment in ICL. There is a scheme for cost-sharing on a fifty-fifty basis in the field of developing hardware and software of an advanced nature; there is the National Computer Centre; and ACTP; and Computer Aided Design Centre—all of these are helping the industry to stay in the forefront of the market.

The result of this co-operation between government and industry was that Britain became one of the only two countries in the world in which IBM, the American hardware manufacturers, hold less than fifty per cent of the computer market.

If this position is to be expanded or even maintained there is an urgent need for ICL to make some critical decisions concerning its top management. The creative and technical team are first-class—as good and better than most other countries have, but much could be done to improve the management side. It is not enough to wait for top management to emerge from the ranks of those presently with the company; what is needed is an active policy of recruitment, even a little lively poaching of outstanding executives from rival companies such as IBM. Some such executives would welcome an approach of this kind as both an opportunity and a challenge.

The quality of management is an essential element in the making of decisions about the future of the industry. For example, the idea of unifying the European-owned computer industry is a good one, but it is rather naïve to try to line up all the companies involved in the hope of getting them to merge their computer interests. A more realistic approach would be to explore the possibility of linking with one international company, and then, if that works successfully, to approach other companies at a later stage. A European computer industry is not the only option open to us at this stage and it is too soon to limit thoughts about the future to this one possibility.

There might also have to be some change in the Government's role of support for the industry. Instead of giving ICL grants, help could be given in the form of development contracts—for example, to develop a machine compatible with both the company's present systems, the system four and the 1900 series, if that is possible.

The government could also do much to stimulate a British "software" industry by putting its own work out to tender among commercial companies rather than maintaining a large force of programmers in its own establishments to do the work needed inside government departments. In the United States even the biggest top security contracts go to outside firms and commercial factors ensure that the government gets good value for money.

The decisions made now are crucial: government policy should be directed towards helping the computer industry expand in the right direction. There is no time to sit back and contemplate past successes complacently.

Carbon Fibres

The third case study is concerned with the manufacture of carbon fibres, a field so new that it can scarcely, as yet, be called an industry.

Carbon fibre has been known for some ninety years, and was used by Swan and Edison for their electric light filament, which was made by carbonizing such things as viscose cellulose, cotton, grasses and bamboo. The exceptionally high theoretical strength and stiffness of long carbon fibre, however, were not achieved until 1963 when a method of manufacturing highly orientated crystallizing fibre involving the controlled carbonization of polyacrylonitrile man-made fibre as the precursor was discovered by the Royal Aircraft Establishment at Farnborough. This process was patented in 1968.

Carbon fibres are not used on their own but are used to reinforce a matrix such as a synthetic resin, metal, ceramic or glass, to form a composite. The principal carbon fibre composites known at present are carbon fibre reinforced plastics (CFRP) which have, for all practical purposes, a higher specific strength and specific stiffness than all other known materials. At present the most widely used reinforced plastics are the strong but light glass fibre reinforced plastics (GRP), developed in 1943 as a result of the need for aircraft radomes. These materials are now used to a considerable extent in building, ship, hovercraft and vehicle construction, chemical plant and general engineering.

The process for making carbon fibre is in four stages, and involves temperatures ranging from 300 degrees Centigrade to 3000 degrees Centigrade. Two types of fibres can be produced— Type I fibre having an exceptionally high stiffness or Type II fibre having an exceptionally high tensile strength. Both types of fibre can be made either as a continuous filament or in short lengths. The final stage of production is to treat the material to develop a surface that can be made to adhere strongly to the ultimate matrix material.

Once the process for making carbon fibres had been developed at Farnborough and patented the patents were, in accordance with the normal practice, handed over to the National Research and Development Corporation, who then became responsible for their exploitation. The Corporation licensed three firms who had, in fact already been in touch with the Royal Aircraft Establishment's work and had acquired a considerable amount of expertise of their own, to produce the fibre. The three firms were Courtaulds, Morgan Crucible, and Rolls-Royce. The Atomic Energy Research Establishment, Harwell, was also brought in to develop larger scale production of carbon fibres than was possible at Farnborough, because they possessed the necessary specialist expertise and equipment for high temperature graphite technology.

Courtaulds' involvement with carbon fibres began in 1963, when the company was asked by the RAE to supply organic fibres suitable for conversion to high quality carbon fibres. To meet this requirement they at first supplied Courtell, later replacing it with a type of acrylic fibre manufactured specifically to meet the Establishment's requirements. The company then built a plant capable of meeting their estimate of demand for this type of acrylic fibre, but this is relatively small by comparison with the type of plant which would be needed for economic production for general purposes and current costs are high. Their principal customers for the precursor material at present are the other licensees, Morgan and Rolls-Royce, and also Harwell and the RAE.

Courtaulds have also built their own plant for the production of carbon fibres, based on the Farnborough technology, and are selling these, under the trade name "Grafil", both in this country and in North America. They have developed processes for treating carbon fibres to enable them to be incorporated in composite materials, and have manufactured plastic mouldings and articles made of plastics reinforced in this way. Initially the company asked the AERE, Harwell, to make Type I fibres for them on a commission basis by graphitization of their own Type II fibres, but they now make both types themselves.

In February 1969, it was announced that an agreement had been completed between Courtaulds and Hercules, Inc. of Wilmington, Delaware, under which Hercules has the exclusive right to sell "Grafil" in the United States and an option to manufacture there at a later date.

Morgan Crucible, the second company to be granted a licence, were brought in at an early stage in the development of carbon fibres because of their knowledge of high temperature technology, which, combined with Courtaulds experience in textiles, the Ministry felt met its requirements in the industrial field. Morgan's first objective was the production of short length fibres, and to this they have now added the production of 1000 ft. lengths. Their principal activity under their licence from NRDC has been the marketing of carbon fibres in the United States, especially within the aerospace industry. An agreement has been concluded with the Whittaker Corporation of Los Angeles which provides for the formation of a joint company for the manufacture of carbon fibres in America. It is expected that the licensing of American firms for the manufacture and marketing of carbon fibres will give a greater financial return than could be expected from the relatively small British aerospace industry, and the agreements provide for access to any technological advances made by the companies concerned. New licensing arrangements also provided for new discoveries made in Britain to be fed into the American market with advantage.

Rolls-Royce, the third company, is in a somewhat different position from Courtaulds and Morgan Crucible. They began to develop gas turbine blades made from glass fibre reinforced plastics in about 1965. When, in 1965, they were sent some carbon fibre from Farnborough and established that carbon fibre reinforced plastic was stronger, lighter and stiffer than G.R.P., they decided to concentrate on the new material, using the experience they had already gained from their work on glass fibre reinforced blades. This meant that, although, in principle, Rolls-Royce were ready to take a licence from the NRDC for the manufacture of carbon fibres once the process was patented, they were not, in fact, interested in the sale of carbon fibres as such. Their interest was in the composites for incorporation in components of their own aero-engines. In 1966 they decided that the only way they could meet the exacting requirements of their own engineers within the requisite time scale and with the necessary degree of commercial security was to develop and build their own carbon fibre plant, and from their own research they produced a composite, "Hyfil", which has already been incorporated into some engines. The company are expecting a progressive increase in the amount of the new material used in their aero-engines.

Rolls-Royce are also engaged, in financial partnership with NRDC, in a materials testing programme, whose object is to extend the use of carbon fibres in materials used for purposes other than aero-engines.

Apart from the work which is being done under licence from the NRDC, there is a two-part programme of the development of high-strength carbon fibres being carried out at Harwell, Farnborough, and elsewhere, under the control of the Directorate of Materials (Aviation) of the Ministry of Technology. This covers both production processes and studies of the engineering uses of composite materials.

The prime role of the Atomic Energy Research Establishment has been the study of the production process, the testing of materials, the study of applications, and the supply of fibres for research and development purposes to both government and industry. It was originally expected that the production of actual fibres at Harwell would soon be rendered unnecessary as a result of industrial firms providing themselves with the requisite plant and facilities, but the Establishment is still receiving requests from industry for supplies of certain types of fibres. It is not, however, intended that Harwell should continue indefinitely as a commercial producer.

The Royal Aircraft Establishment at Farnborough continues to work in association with Harwell and to give assistance to industry, either under contract or by the handing out of information, in finding engineering applications for carbon fibre composites.

The role of NRDC is to exploit and develop inventions of publicly-supported bodies. Their first action, in this case, as we have seen, was to license the three companies whose activities have been described, although there has been some delay in the actual signing of the licensing agreements. The Corporation and the companies found some difficulty in agreeing on the matter of payments; NRDC are obliged to cover their own expenses to some extent and wished to make a reasonable charge, but, at the same time, they did not wish to prejudice the public interest by charging so much that the licensees were unable to negotiate effectively with American companies.

In February 1969, the Select Committee on Science and Technology reported on the state of development[1] and in so doing, pin-pointed the problem which is central to this whole question of industries of innovation and the relationship between government and industry:

"A technological advance of the greatest importance has been made by government scientists. The advent of carbon fibre reinforced plastics, metals, ceramics and glass may well influence the entire practice of engineering on a vaster scale than any previously developed new material. How then is the nation to reap the maximum benefit without it becoming yet another British invention to be exploited more successfully or more fully overseas?"[2]

In the context of carbon fibres the answer can be specific. It is clearly of far greater advantage to this country in terms of net return if products having a very high added value, like aircraft engines, are exported rather than just carbon fibres.

Because of the very considerable experience of industry in the United States in the use of fibre reinforced composites and the development by Union Carbide of boron reinforced composites and Thornel carbon fibre there is no possibility of

[1] H.C. Paper 157 (1968–9).
[2] Paragraph 36.

excluding American firms from the market. It is therefore obviously to the advantage of this country if agreements made between British and American firms ensure a feedback of American know-how on the applications of fibre composites, and this has been the policy of NRDC, but it is difficult to ensure this. The Ministry of Technology has felt some anxiety over passing on this general know-how, as distinct from information relating to the manufacturing process, because there is no restraint on firms whose principle interest is in the sale of carbon fibres, or as in the case of Courtaulds, carbon fibres and its precursor material, because the only effect the passing on of composite know-how will have will be to enlarge the market for the fibre and precursor material. In the case of a firm such as Rolls-Royce, however, whose principal interest is the manufacture of end-products based on CFRP, composite know-how will only be passed on to any of their American associates if it helps to promote their overall commercial interest. Composite know-how from government establishments should be made available only to those firms actually investing in the manufacture of end products based on carbon fibre, so that commercial restraints will apply to their exchanges of information with American associates. Furthermore, the decision as to which firms should have access to the composite know-how, as opposed to the fibre manufacturing process, should rest with the government establishments concerned and not with the NRDC.

I would recommend the setting up of a large scale carbon fibre plant. While recognising that there is a commercial risk in establishing a large plant before the demand materials, there are two strong arguments in doing this. First, the scale of production has a big effect on the cost of the fibres and, if wide-scale work on the development of end products is to be stimulated, a lower price carbon fibre must be available at once. Secondly, most countries already have a major reinforced plastics industry, based on glass fibre, so that the future size and course of the market for carbon fibre is not completely unpredictable.

There are three ways of achieving the building of such a

plant: that the three licensees jointly invest in such a plant; that the NRDC look for an additional licensee who would be prepared to take the risk of building a plant based on the latest design study from Harwell; and that the Atomic Energy Authority set up their own plant (and should in any case have a financial interest in any large scale plant built). Action is required soon, otherwise our lead in the carbon fibre field will soon disappear lost, not to the Americans, but to the Japanese, who have not only signed a cross-licensing agreement with the NRDC, relating to the patents held by each company so far as the carbonization of polyacrylonitrile is concerned, but have also begun commercial production of carbon fibres based on hydrocarbons, a process unrelated to that carried out at the Royal Aircraft Establishment, which is the subject of the agreement.

Conclusions

The development of the computer industry, demonstrates that the idea of a fruitful partnership between government and industry is not a mere pipe-dream. It can be a reality. If the same constructive approach had been evident in the nuclear power industry, and the very relevant recommendations of the Select Committee followed up, we might well have had a similar success story. The ingredients were much the same: in both fields British technological skill gave a lead over the rest of the world; in both cases, established companies had to learn the commercial application of new techniques; in both cases, the financial risk was such that reorganisation of the companies involved and government assistance were necessary. Why then did the recipe produce such different results in the two industries?

The main reason why the nuclear power industry has failed to realise its potential, especially in the export market, may well lie in the nature of its early success. The growing industry of the 1950s found itself alone in the home market; most of its research and development work was carried out by a government agency, the Atomic Energy Authority, which licensed its patents to the consortia; the high development costs of this research were also borne by the government; at the time when the first nuclear power programme was planned, coal supplies were limited, so that the nuclear power industry found itself from the first with a virtually captive customer in the shape of the electricity generating boards. The government's interest in the industry stemmed mainly from its interest in increasing Britain's power resources at an economic price.

This policy was, no doubt, at the time the right one. But neither the government nor the industry appear to have recognized the moment when circumstances changed; the moment when they should have widened their horizons. One can only suspect that they had become too complacent. The least satisfied party seems to be the customer. The Central Electricity Board, for instance, thought that there would be a considerable saving in development costs if, instead of complete designs being produced by the tendering consortia, nuclear power stations had their layouts designed by the CEGB, as do conventional power stations, allowing manufacturers to design and tender for individual components. The need for greater competition in the industry is undeniable; the competition already exists in the export market and one is led to speculate how long it will be before foreign companies become genuinely competitive in the home market if the home industry fails to recognize the need for change.

The computer industry was born into a highly competitive world and this stimulated its rapid growth; the need to fight for its home market enabled it to see from the beginning that it had to set its sights on the international market. The industry was, perhaps, fortunate in that the moment when it was ready to develop coincided with the moment when technological advance became, for a time, a political war cry, but that is not the whole story. No doubt the fact that only one Ministry was involved, and that a new, enthusiastic one, helped in developing a clear policy, whereas the nuclear power industry has hovered somewhere between two ministries throughout its existence. The transfer of the functions of the Ministry of

Power to the Ministry of Technology should help to create a more unified approach.

The main lesson to be learned, however, seems to be that both sides must show a great deal more intelligence and imagination. Successful programmes, such as the nuclear power industry had in the 1950s, must be constantly re-examined, by both industry and government. As the home market becomes steadily less able to support competition in those industries where the high cost of research and development lead to ever more mergers, government must give industry every encouragement to launch out into the international market, and provide advice and assistance to enable it to compete effectively with its rivals abroad. And it is important that research and development should be continuous : there is already a cloud on the success of the British computer industry, for it seems likely that the development of a large British-designed computer may come too late for the British industry to obtain the same share of the market, *vis-à-vis* the Americans, as it has with the smaller machines.

Nevertheless, to date, the development of the computer industry is a model to be studied; but just as many lessons may be learned from the failure of government and industry to act in partnership in the nuclear power industry.

The experience of the nuclear power industry is very relevant to the as yet unfinished story of carbon fibres. These case studies demonstrate that there is no shortage either of new ideas or of the technological know-how needed to develop them. Where the government-industry partnership fails is in bringing industrial innovations to the point at which they are commercially viable in time to reap the maximum benefit from them in international markets. If the experience of the computer industry can be regarded as typical, it would appear that this break in the chain from invention to commercial production is less likely to occur when the initiative comes from industry than when it comes from government. Government is better equipped to respond to the stated needs of industry than it is to initiate

the commercial development of inventions made in government laboratories.

The need of greater flexibility so that government establishments enter into direct commercial relationships with outside firms is confirmed in two reports. The Central Advisory Council for Science and Technology's report "Technological Innovation in Britain" argued that one of the factors which makes for success in technological innovation is, "the direct linkage of the research and development activities to the general manufacturing, financial, and marketing activities of the organization as a whole". The second report, that of the Select Committee, includes the evidence not only of the industrialists but also of the government's scientists from Harwell, who felt that there was conflict here with the present role of the NRDC.[1]

The role of NRDC has been described as that of a "marriage broker", going round looking for new ideas and introducing them to industry. The role was rather more complex in the case of carbon fibres, as the initial contact between the research establishments and industry had already been made, and their principal function was the drawing up of the licensing agreements, in which they have considerable expertise, necessary because of the interest of the United States in the aero-space field. But although they have funds available to assist industry in developing new ideas to commercial viability, they cannot do any more than influence the course of events. The NRDC cannot control industry's choice as to which ideas it will follow up, and while it may be very persuasive, its role as liaison between research scientists and industrialists may well be a hindrance rather than a help. If government research is to be fully exploited commercially for the benefit of the nation it must be exploited through commercial channels which industrialists recognize as such. The alternatives are the national corporation, which has now been adopted in the case of nuclear fuel and radio isotopes, free to raise money in the commercial

[1]H.C. Paper 157, para 16. Select Committee on Carbon Fibres, HMSO, 1969.

market, and direct contracts for industrial development with private industry.

In this context it is interesting to examine, briefly, the Ministry of Technology's proposals for reorganising government research. It is proposed[1] to reorganize government laboratories (with the exception of the Royal Radar and Royal Aircraft Establishments) together with the NRDC into a new statutory corporation, the British Research and Development Corporation. Its aims and functions would be:

(i) to encourage and support the development and application of innovation and technological improvement in industry for the benefit of the UK economy; and to carry out research and development for this purpose, both itself and in collaboration with industry and on repayment;

(ii) to carry out research programmes necessary in the public interest, including basic research, and other specific programmes of work required by government departments and other public authorities;

(iii) to exploit where appropriate innovations resulting from government financed programmes carried out by other agencies.

It is only the first of these aims which really concerns us here; the third, although relevant, is simply a continuation of the present work of the NRDC. What is new is the contractual approach to research and development, which will apply not only to work done for industry, but also all work done for government departments. This approach will give BRDC greater freedom in its relationship with industry than any of the research establishments have at present, and will enable the Corporation to engage in joint ventures with industry, sharing costs and risks. Industrial participation is regarded by the Ministry as the simplest test of the value to industry of work in government establishments. While it is not possible to estimate

[1]*Industrial Research and Development in Government Laboratories.*

exactly how much of such work industry would want, a research and development organisation which would live to a large extent on its earnings from contracts, joint ventures, royalty arrangements, and the like would have its level of operations determined to a large extent by its success in meeting the needs of industry. Such success would, the Ministry thinks, make it possible to reduce the level of government subsidy for industrial research, and the extent and nature of such work undertaken in government laboratories would thus be increasingly determined by industry itself.

This is certainly one way of ensuring that there is a direct linkage between research and development and general industrial production and marketing. But there seems to be a danger that industry may not use the research facilities offered by the government, preferring to use its own. In 1966–7 companies spent some £37 million outside their own laboratories, £19 million of it with other companies, £10 million in research associations, and only £6.5 million in government laboratories (as compared with government's own expenditure of £180 million). If industry alone initiates areas of research, resulting in the application of strictly commercial attitudes from the beginning, there is a strong possibility that future research will be too limited in scope. Commercial factors are more properly applicable to the post-research stage, when there is an actual product to be developed and marketed.

Nor is it at all clear that carbon fibres, for instance, would have fared any better if the new Corporation had already been in existence. It is not enough that the results of government research should be made available to industry to develop if it wants to. Government must be able to initiate commercial development either by entering into commercial agreements with industry or by the formation of commercial corporations able to raise money in both the public and private sectors. Present procedures are too slow. To quote further from the Central Advisory Council report on "Technological Innovation in Britain" : "Given a decision to go ahead with a new development, a short lead-time is equally essential. One reason for this is purely economic. Innovation costs money. The shorter the time between the start of a project and its commercial fulfilment, the sooner the commercial returns." Where existing companies are unable or unwilling to bring about this commercial fulfilment, new companies can be created by the government. This should already have been done with carbon fibres.

Not all innovation comes from government laboratories nor even from the laboratories of large international companies. Government's approach to the sponsorship of innovation should extend to small companies, and NRDC's funds are, to some extent, used for this purpose. But such small companies are to a very large degree financed by the private investor and since research and development costs can lead to very large losses, something should be done to encourage private investment in such small research-based companies. The American approach is to allow losses on such investments to be set off against income, rather than, as is done in this country, to restrict such set off to investment gains only. The result can be that actual loss is reduced to as little as thirty per cent. The consequence in America has been the fast growth of companies such as Xerox, which are the envy of the world. The ambivalent attitude of the Labour Party towards the private investor and unearned income may make it difficult for a similar approach to be adopted under a Labour government, but it is at least arguable that the incidence of a few more millionaires would be a small price to pay for a crop of fast-growing industries of innovation.

If the partnership of industry and government is to flourish in this area of innovation, the two sectors need to start working together on the earlier stages of project development. It is not enough to hope that government will become more commercially-minded and industry more research-orientated. Our case-histories show that both parties are needed, but often there is a complete lack of trust. It is up to government, in most cases, to take the initiative. Only in this way can the technical opportunities of the future—cryogenics, oceanography, lasers, and the rest—be used to their full advantage.

6

MAKING GOVERNMENT MORE EFFECTIVE

I SUGGESTED EARLIER that one of the main causes of strain in the relationship between government and industry has been the failure of government to be effective in its own terms. "Effective government" in the context of government-industry relations means a government which is capable of identifying objectives relevant to the best use of the nation's resources, of formulating the policies necessary to the attainment of these objectives, and of seeing that they are carried out.

So far as the actual structure of government is concerned, I am convinced that it is more than time for a moratorium between the political parties, restricting any further redistribution or re-arrangement of functions between departments. If government is to function efficiently, the departments must now be allowed a period in which to identify their allotted tasks and discover the best ways to carry them out. In fact, the allocation of functions now in operation corresponds quite closely to the Haldane Committee recommendations, allowing for the enormous growth in the nature of government responsibilities.

The size of the Cabinet and the actual numbers of Ministers, however, are, of course, very much larger than the Haldane Committee recommended. But, if the device of the "Inner Cabinet" is taken into consideration, and the multiple responsibilities of most of its members, it can be seen that, in fact, an attempt has been made to reach a compromise in what, as Richard Rose points out,[1] is a very real dilemma :

"If [the Cabinet] is small, a dozen men or less, all of whom are 'co-ordinating' ministers, then communication within the

[1]*People in Politics,* Faber, 1970.

group will be good, but communication between the group and those responsible for administering specific departments will suffer. Reciprocally, if communication between ministers and operational executives is good, the time available for co-ordination is constricted."

While it cannot be claimed that the Labour Government's structure resolved this conflict, it may have held the key to the solution. Between the "Inner Cabinet" of "co-ordinating ministers" and the junior ministers who are responsible for the day-to-day operation of the departments, lay the full Cabinet, who provided an overlap in the system of communications.

And if government is to be effective the two-way flow of communication between government and industry must be as free as possible from distortion. The channel of communication is the Civil Service.

The Civil Service

Government as it reaches the governed is a matter of administration rather than of politics, and, no matter which party is in office, the administrators remain the same. The British have long boasted, with justification, of the incorruptibility of their Civil Service : it is only in recent years that it has been questioned whether incorruptibility is the sole virtue required of a civil servant.

In government's relationships with industry, the part played by the Civil Service, especially in such areas as the administration of financial aid and incentives, goes far beyond what is normally meant by "administration". As long as governments saw their role as one of action only when action was unavoidable, the ability to execute policies was enough. Now that it often falls to governments to initiate action, the Civil Service has, and has had for some time, a larger role to play. It is the Civil Service which must collect, assimilate and present the data on which governments formulate their policies; it is the Civil Service which must implement the schemes set in motion by the government, a process which demands the ability to make

value judgements, to interpret data, and, in the industrial context especially, the ability to maintain good relationships with
the private sector and the trade unions. In the quality of the
administrators lies, very often, the success or failure of a
policy.

Professor André Bertrand of the Ecole Nationale d'Administration, Paris, has described the higher civil servant as "the social
scientist in action".[1] The questions which must be asked are,
"Are our civil servants properly recruited and trained for this
work? Are they qualified to fulfil the tasks set? How do they
compare with their equivalents in other countries? What can be
done to remedy their defects?"

It is not easy to assess the precise state of the British Civil
Service today. The publication of the Fulton Report on the
Civil Service in 1968[2] set in motion changes in the training and
organization of the Service. It will be some time before the
extent and effect of these changes becomes known outside the
"corridors of power". A consideration of the history of the
Civil Service, insofar as it affects its present structure, and of
the findings of the Fulton Committee would, however, be in
order in the context of the present study.

Origin of the Civil Service

The Civil Service as we know it today is a nineteenth-century
development. The earliest jobs were the subject of patronage :
originally handed out by the Crown, they were "freehold" and
could be bought, sold, bequeathed or occupied by a deputy;
they carried a salary or fees but did not always involve any work,
and if for any reason an office was abolished, its occupier was
compensated. The patronage system began to break down towards the end of the eighteenth century, under pressure of
public opinion, led by the Benthamites from outside, and
through the increase of actual work from the inside. By the end

[1]W. A. Robson, ed., *The Civil Service in Britain and France,* Hogarth
Press, 1966, p.175.
[2]Cmnd. 3638.

of the late 1830s the money paid out for service to the government had more relevance to the work done, but there was still no central organization for government servants who were employed by individual Ministers and paid out of the money voted to each department.

Attention was focused on the system, or rather lack of it, during the period of the Crimean War by, among others, Florence Nightingale and the war correspondent of *The Times*, who revealed that there were seven different departments involved in the army organization. It also became known that changes of government meant changes in paid officials.

But already Sir Charles Trevelyan, a former employee of the East India Company's civil administration in India, a service run by the Company on behalf of the Crown, and then employed as Assistant Under-Secretary to the Treasury, and Sir Stafford Northcote, formerly Private Secretary to Gladstone, had been asked to report and make recommendations on the organization of the public service. Their report (in which the term "Civil Service" is used for the first time in this context) was published in 1853. Its stated objects were "to provide . . . for the supply of the public service with a thoroughly efficient class of men, to encourage industry and foster merit . . . and to mitigate the evils which result from the fragmentary nature of the service."

They found that there was no guarantee of promotion or other incentive for persons of ability to join the public service, especially as the rate of pay was low. They recommended that selection for the service should be by competitive examination and that there should be a separation of "intellectual" work from routine work, which at that stage involved a good deal of copying. They recommended that civil servants should be sufficiently independent to be able to advise and even influence Ministers.

It was as a result of the Northcote-Trevelyan Report that the Civil Service Commissioners were appointed to organize recruitment along the lines suggested. Thus came into existence the

Administrative and Clerical Divisions of the Service, to be followed some time later by the Executive Division, with direct entry into each class and little movement between.

The size of the Civil Service has grown with the expansion of government departments already considered in Chapter 2, from about 53,000 in 1871 to about three-quarters of a million today. In 1919 the Civil Service National Whitley Council was set up to deal with conditions of service on the basis of joint negotiations, but the Civil Service had already shown its strength in the previous year when the pull of departmental interests had effectively negatived many of the restructuring proposals of the Haldane Committee. Pre-eminent in strength was the Treasury, claiming, by right of a tradition which it seems to have established itself, the position of head of the Civil Service for its own departmental head, and the right to issue regulations concerning the external activities and conduct of civil servants.

Largely as a result of the personalities involved, the competitive examination for entry into the Administrative class of the Civil Service was, from the first, weighted in favour of graduates in the humanities from Oxford or Cambridge who, in their own selection procedures, themselves favoured the products of the resurgent public schools. Thus, as Max Nicholson, one of the strongest critics of the present Civil Service, points out, began the cult of the amateur in English public life. Of the effects of this cult he says:

What is not often appreciated, however, is that a negative process is at work in the selection of civil servants. As schoolboys they must fail to show enough individuality and initiative to fall foul of the powers that be, as a fair minority of the ablest boys do. As undergraduates at university they must fail to show the type of keen interest in any learned subject leading them into one of the degree courses which frown on, because they were long frowned on by, the Civil Service. They must equally fail to show promise for a higher degree, which would probably lead to their staying on as university teachers or researchers, or would at best handicap them by having to arrange a long deferment of their Civil Service entry behind their more carefree contemporaries who join immediately on graduating. They must, too, fail to attract the insistent notice of the countless talent scouts of large industry who comb the universities first for much the same levels of ability sought by the Civil Service, but with more accent on enterprise and leadership. They must then fail to recognise, as many of the brighter undergraduates do, that entering the present-day Civil Service can prove more frustrating than several alternative choices. Having thus reached the qualifying score they present themselves as candidates to the Civil Service Commission, who, in accepting them for the profession of public administration, will sanctify by a cock-hat certificate, their failure to acquire any professional qualification and their admission to a profession which indeed looks up to leaders glorifying in the conviction that no such profession exists.[1]

The criticism is humorous, but it is also damning. To see that it is also true it is necessary to look no further than the Report of the Fulton Committee on the Civil Service.

The Fulton Report

The Fulton Report opens with this remarkable statement:

The Home Civil Service today is still fundamentally the product of the nineteenth century philosophy of the North-cote-Trevelyan Report. The task it faces are those of the second half of the twentieth century.

Specifically, the Report points out that too few civil servants are trained managers; that scientists, engineers and other specialists do not carry the weight of authority to which their expertise should entitle them; that the careers structure, petrified as it is into classes and allowing very little movement, either on temporary exchange or on a permanent basis, between

[1] Max Nicholson, *The System,* Hodder, 1967.

the Service and outside employers, is out of date; and there is too little contact between the service and the community.

All these criticisms might have been expected; what is perhaps more surprising to those without detailed knowledge of Civil Service recruiting procedures, is the extent to which the nature of the personnel employed has remained the same throughout all the social changes of this century. While the universities, local government and industry have reflected the changes in the social structure in the world at large, the Civil Service, according to the Social Survey instigated by the Fulton Committee, has remained virtually unchanged. The proportion of "exclusive" middle class direct entrants into the administrative Class, educated at public schools and Oxbridge (over 60 per cent) had hardly declined from its pre-war level, and was still largely concentrated in the arts and humanities (71 per cent) rather than the social sciences.

A detailed examination of the modern tasks which the Service is called upon to perform led the Committee to suggest one simple guiding principle for the future—"Look at the job first", and in the light of this principle to "continuously review the tasks it is called upon to perform and the possible ways in which it may perform them; it should then consider what new skills and kinds of men and women are needed and how they can be found".

The adoption of this principle would require a major change in recruitment policy and training procedures, which would need to be redesigned with the aim of finding the best man for each particular job, rather than the best man to fit into the system. The Committee recommended that, to meet the demands made by modern governments on the Civil Service, control of the Service should pass from the Treasury to a new Civil Service Department, responsible directly to the Prime Minister.

Recognising the need for greater professionalism among both specialist and administrative staff, the Committee recommended that the selection of graduate entrants to administrative work should be deliberately weighted in favour of those whose university studies had been in subjects thought closely relevant to

Civil Service work.[1] A Civil Service College should be set up to provide major training courses in administration, not only for recruits to the Service at graduate and other levels, but also additional courses for those moving into top management, and refresher courses to keep the Service abreast of new developments in management techniques. The College should also have research functions. The Report recommended that the College when set up should put in hand a rapid and large scale programme for the further training of the *present* generation of civil servants.[2]

Finally, in the interest of efficiency, the Committee recommended techniques such as O & M, the "problem-solving" approach to organisation, the number of working levels in the hierarchy, and so on, be applied to the work of departments.

It is interesting to note that, fifty years earlier, the Haldane Committee Report had made similar recommendations, when they hoped that in all departments better provisions would be made for enquiry, research and reflection before policy was defined and put into operation; that for some purposes the necessary research would be carried out by a Department of Government specially charged with these duties, and that in all departments the higher officials would have more time to devote to research and reflection. The hope was only partly fulfilled, and we are, as a result, fifty years behindhand in acquiring a "purpose-built" Civil Service.

Civil Servants Abroad

The Fulton recommendation that the United Kingdom Civil Service should move to a unified grading structure has been accepted, and a study of the structure is in progress. As a preliminary step a team was sent to study the civil services of Canada and the United States.[3]

The team found that the Canadian Civil Service is "job-oriented"; rank and classification reside in the job and not, as

[1]Recommendation 24.
[2]Recommendations 38–51.
[3]*The Civil Services of North America*, HMSO, 1969.

is the tendency in this country, in the man. Individuals are recruited at all levels to fill specific posts rather than to join a service. This means that, while the general pattern is to recruit graduates fresh from university, there is a good deal of recruitment above the "entrance level": for example, some 15 per cent of appointments to the Executive Category (which covers the top six hundred jobs) are made direct from the private sector.

The basis of the structure is the traditional North American preference for free enterprise. Employers are not expected to manage the careers of their employees; what they are expected to do is to make it easy for employees to move on their own initiative, by widespread advertisement of vacancies, the holding of multiple competitions to ensure a fair chance for all comers, and by acceptance of the principle by all concerned that an employer does not seek to hinder a man's movement to another job. The principle also allows the poaching of staff from other departments.

This traditional approach, though theoretically it might seem to ensure that each job is occupied by the best man for it, has not proved adequate to meet the problems of running a modern Civil Service. The rate of movement tends to be too fast to allow for depth of experience; at the same time it prevents personnel acquiring experience in fields of work for which they are not formally qualified but in which they need experience to fit them for broad policy-making and management posts at the top of the Service. The Canadians have therefore begun to move away from free movement towards a policy of planned placement.

In order to identify and train future members of the Executive Category, the Canadians have devised a *Career Assignment Programme*. Candidates are identified and selected by their Departments; they are then sent on a three-month training course, followed by assignment to another Department for two years; after a spell in their home Department they go out again, often to a job outside the central government. Finally they return to their original Department to take up an "executive" position. The Departments are thus able to do some long-range career planning, knowing that they will themselves benefit from the training given, while the candidates are able to acquire the non-specialist experience necessary without jeopardising their careers.

The "executive" training course is one of the few central training courses run by the Public Service Commission. Much of the training is given by the Departments themselves, on the principle that training should be close to where the action is. In addition, external training by the universities, either by participation in their normal courses or in specially constructed courses, is purchased. There is no central Civil Service College.

The United States Federal Service is run on very similar lines, with one important difference : that is, that the appointments at the top of the Service are "political" and therefore, subject to change on a change of administration. In fact, they do not all change hands at this time; it is becoming increasingly common for career civil servants to move up into non-career posts, and there is a strong tendency to appoint to these posts only those who have appropriate qualifications and experience for the job. Nevertheless, the break in the career structure is important because it provides a real limit to the distance a career civil servant can travel and still retain security of tenure; and it provides little incentive to Departments to develop career civil servants with the breadth of experience and insight that are needed by the top administrator. Hitherto, the ideal career civil servant has been seen as the specialist working in support of the non-career generalist.

Recently, however, the Federal Service has developed the Executive Assignment System, with the object of producing a corps of mobile, trained administrators who could co-ordinate and weld together a government-wide approach to the disparate aims and programmes of the multiple organs of the Executive. The system is still in its early stages, and it is not yet clear whether it will really produce administrators with a broad approach or whether, if it does, the system will adapt to provide jobs for a common corps of senior staff in the career structure.

The system now has a training arm in the shape of the Federal Executive Institute, which runs short courses for the higher grade civil servants in the behavioural sciences, and the problems of managing large groups and gives them experience in the complexity of major contemporary problems.

By contrast with the North American civil services the European civil services have always aimed primarily at building up a career service on a professional basis. Personnel are recruited either, as in France, Belgium and Italy, by competitive examination, or as in Sweden, Finland, Switzerland, Holland, Portugal, Denmark, Germany and Norway, by a comparison of the paper qualifications already possessed by the candidate. Once recruited, it is commonly accepted throughout Europe that further training is necessary for specialist public servants. Some countries, such as Switzerland, reject all training for administrators; those countries which accept the need for training administrators adopt one of three methods : pre-entry training under state auspices, which may not guarantee actual entry to the service; full or part-time training after entry in a state institution; refresher courses for civil servants with some seniority, designed to widen their experience. The German Länder illustrate the first method, the training programme falling into three stages; first the university final examination in law; followed by a long period of service in various departments of public administration; the final stage is a state examination. The principal advantage of the system is that it provides a common background for all the higher officials in the public service, whether lawyers or administrators, as well as the private legal system; it also provides some recruits for private industry. The insistence on the legal qualification does, however, lose the flexibility which acceptance of candidates from a wider variety of disciplines would offer. An even more serious criticism is that the length of the pre-entry training, three-and-a-half years, leads to an excessively bureaucratic approach in even the youngest civil servants.

The French Civil Service offers the most successful example of a system operating the principle of post-entry training. The

Service has long accepted the principle for specialist public servants, and since 1945, has extended it to its administrators in the foundation of the Ecole Nationale d'Administration. There are two parallel entrance examinations to the School : one for graduates (no longer limited, as in the past, to law graduates), and one for those who have already had five years in the public service in any capacity. The training lasts for nearly three years : the first is spent away from Paris assisting in general administration in the provinces (local government is part of the same public service structure); the second year is spent at the School, learning administrative principles and techniques and languages; the next stage is a period of two months spent working for a private firm, industrial or commercial; the final period is spent, partly at the School and partly in the Department to which they are assigned, learning the actual job. As with the German pre-entry training the principal criticism must be the length of training, tending towards the creation of a monolithic public service. The periods of experience in the provinces and in outside industry must, however, have some effect in countering this tendency.

Refresher courses for senior civil servants seem to be the accepted practice throughout Europe, though only Britain and France to date have institutions specially designed to give this training. No country can so far be said to have achieved unqualified success with its training schemes; the difficulties involved in releasing staff and in getting them to take the courses seriously and settle to study have mitigated against total success.

So far as career structure is concerned, in all countries civil servants have great security of tenure, in most cases with little or no movement between the various branches of the administration, and little movement between the public service and private undertakings.

What can be learned from the experience of other countries? The experience of the North American civil services suggests that a career structure, albeit less rigid than the present one, is desirable if the public service is to attract the most able men for its top jobs. Recruitment by competitive examination is probably a more just system than recruitment on the basis of existing qualifications, but it should not be assumed that, given the complexities of the modern state, administration can be learned on the job; on the other hand, too long a training may result in too rigid an outlook. It is interesting to note in this context that Professor André Bertrand, comparing the recruitment and training of higher civil servants in the United Kingdom and France, showed a slight preference for the British method of testing the candidate as a whole (Method II) but thought that the British must eventually set up a professional institute or training centre.[1]

While, therefore, much can be learned from European examples on recruitment and training, it is to North America we must look for example in integrating the techniques of modern management into the public service, and providing a two-way exchange of personnel, and ideas, between the public and private sector.

After Fulton

It can hardly be said, writing a year later, that the publication of the Fulton Report has led to any major changes in the Civil Service, certainly not to any that are apparent to the outsider.

The Prime Minister announced on the day of publication that the government accepted the proposal to establish a new Civil Service Department, which has accepted the Fulton principle of "look at the job first",[2] but it will be some time before it becomes clear whether the Civil Service has accepted all that follows from this principle.

On recruitment and training there have been two important developments. First, the proposal for a Civil Service College has been accepted by the government; unfortunately, its timing is dependent on a programme taking full account of public

[1] W. A. Robson, ed., *The Civil Service in Britain and France,* Chapter 14.
[2] *Developments on Fulton,* Civil Service National Whitley Council, February 1969.

expenditure control. It is difficult to comprehend the apparent absence of any real sense of urgency in this matter; it must surely be realised that a really efficient Civil Service, such as it is hoped a fully trained Service would be, must make a significant contribution to the control of public expenditure. The saving to the public purse if such failures of Civil Service know-how as the scandalous over-pricing of defence contracts in recent years can be avoided would more than outweigh the cost of such an establishment.

Secondly, October 1969 saw the publication of the Report of the Committee of Inquiry into Civil Service Selection Procedures,[1] set up on the recommendation of the Fulton Committee to consider the implications of the Social Survey, referred to above. The complacency of this report in the light of both Fulton and the Social Survey is astonishing. For example :

"No other post-war development in the field of personnel selection in this country has had so strong and so pervasive an influence and there are few, if any, equally advanced procedures for selecting potential managers or administrators which have not derived wholly or in part from Method II. It has supplied the Civil Service with recruits of whom only a very small proportion indeed are of less than the required quality."

Concerning the high proportion of entrants from social classes I and II (79 per cent) and from the Universities of Oxford and Cambridge, the Committee found no evidence of bias on the part of the selection boards, and concluded that "The make-up of the entry reflected the character of the field of candidates who chose to compete rather than the choice made by the selectors". There are several points to be made here.

First, while there may be no conscious bias in favour of Oxbridge graduates with middle-class backgrounds the fact that, for example, other universities gained only 41 per cent of the successes while supplying 65 per cent of the candidates in 1968 suggests at least a subconscious bias. Secondly, when the prevailing image in the outside world is that the entry *is* biased in this way, a high proportion of potential entrants from other

[1]Cmnd. 4156.

universities will opt out by simply not bothering to apply in the first place. Equally, as Max Nicholson pointed out in the extract already quoted, an examination of the present workings of the Civil Service may well suggest to the undergraduate and potential recruit that a career in that service would be a frustrating affair. The Fulton Report suggests that he would probably be right. In other words, while, as the Committee concludes, the best candidates may be being selected, it does not necessarily follow that the candidates themselves are the best that can be found.

Further, while it is true that the Civil Services Method II selection procedure has, in many respects, led the way in this country in the use of, for example, psychological tests, the great importance still attached to the assessment of personality involves some considerable degree of subjectivity. However fair-minded the selection boards may be consciously, as long as the results show a preference for candidates from particular social backgrounds, the suspicion will remain that like selects like. The result is that future generations of civil servants will suffer from the same limitations as the one with which the country is expressing its dissatisfaction.

The predominance of middle-class recruits to the Civil Service does, however, seem to be endemic to the nature of the Service, being also true of the United States and France. It may not, therefore, be wholly disastrous, although it must inevitably act as a block in the chain of communication between government and governed. What does militate against a real change in the nature and efficiency of the Civil Service is the very low proportion of new entrants who graduate in any subject outside the arts and humanities. It is regrettable that the Fulton recommendation of "preference for relevance"[1] has been rejected by the government on the grounds that it is difficult to identify "relevant" subjects, and easier to identify "relevant" individuals who, once identified, can be trained as required. The effect of rejecting this principle will surely be to discourage graduates in other subjects to apply for entry to the Civil Service, as well as

[1]Recommendation 24.

ensuring that students who take their degrees with entrance to the Civil Service in mind continue to look no further than the liberal arts for their studies.

The recommendations of the Fulton Committee on the structure of the Service, on conditions of employment and on mobility seem to have been accepted in principle, although most of them are still a matter for study rather than the subject of any action. In July 1969 the Whitley Council published a statement on the timing of interim changes in the grading structure of the service. In March 1970 it was announced that, beginning in January 1971 there will be an open structure at top levels of the Civil Service in which each post is filled by the individual best fitted for it, regardless of his profession, discipline and previous history within the Service. All classes will be abolished and a single rationalized pay and grading structure substituted. This is in line with the Fulton recommendation that "there are strong arguments for preserving a mainly career service in the sense that most civil servants should enter when comparatively young with the expectation, but not the guarantee, of a lifetime's employment." In addition, greater efforts are now being made to arrange two-way interchanges between the Civil Service, industry and commerce on a short-term basis. Movement in and out of the Service on a more permanent basis is increasing but not much progress has been made so far towards solving the problems such mobility presents, not only within the Service but throughout industry, so far as such fringe, but to the older recruit, essential benefits as pension rights are concerned.

The Fulton Committee doubted whether, in the past, the Service had been sufficiently tough in dealing with inefficiency in its ranks. There seems to be no doubt that the concept of "establishment" has, in practice, offered much protection to those who achieved it. Fulton recommend that compulsory early retirement "in the interests of the Service" should be made possible. The principle seems to have been accepted, but once again the matter is under study. Now that the doctrine of Ministerial responsibility for the acts of the Civil Service seems to have fallen into disuse, in that a Minister is no longer required

to resign for the misdeeds of the civil servants under his command, some other safeguard for the public interest is required,
and it is right that civil servants should be required to accept
a greater degree of personal responsibility for their acts and
omissions.

It seems likely that if the recommendations of the Fulton
Committee are accepted, in spirit as well as letter, the quality of
the personnel may improve, with the reservations already stated,
and they should be better trained for the work which they
are called upon to perform. The Fulton Report does, therefore,
represent a significant step forward in the modernisation of
government.

It must, however, be remembered that the management of the
Civil Service is not an end in itself, and it is the realisation of
this that leads to the recommendations of the Fulton Committee on the use of modern management techniques in public
administration. It is, for example, useless to depend on an
inquiry into government organization approximately every 30
years, as has been the case in the past. Progressive businesses
in the private sector conduct such inquiries every two to three
years in order to maintain efficient operations.

The adoption by industry of social science techniques—in
conditioning personnel policies and industrial relations practice,
for example, make the acceptance of such techniques by government a matter of some urgency. Government, as we have seen,
is encroaching more and more on the preserves of industry and
exerting an ever-increasing influence on staff, employment and
personnel policies. Unless government both understands and, in
its own organization and decision-making, accepts the modern
approaches to which the social sciences give rise, there can be no
meaningful dialogue between government and industry.

This is an area in which there is much to be learned from
the United States, where there has been positive action-research,
with politicians and researchers constantly making appraisals as
to the most effective way of using the social scientist in government service and of providing a constant feedback from the
researcher to the policy-maker. The recent publication of the

United States Department of Health, Education and Welfare, *Towards a Social Report,* is an instructive example.

In March 1966 President Johnson directed the Secretary for Health, Education and Welfare "to research for ways to improve the nation's ability to chart its social progress". The aim of the study, of which the report is the outcome, was to develop the necessary social indications which would measure social change and also help to establish goals. The first step towards this was for the Secretary of the Department to invite a group of leading social scientists to advise on ways of measuring social changes and the possibility of preparing a social report. The social scientists and representatives of the Department then attempted to discover ways in which an annual assessment of social well-being could be achieved. The actual report was prepared by the Department, but teams of social scientists worked with the government officials.

The basic aim was stated as the preparation of "A social report with a set of social indicators [which] could not only satisfy our curiosity about how well we are doing, but . . . also improve public policy-making." The document they prepared attempts to establish indicators to assess how successful the United States has been in progressing towards generally accept-able goals. The areas in which they endeavoured to set up these social indicators are health and illness, social mobility, the con-dition of the physical environment, income and poverty, public order and safety, learning, science and art. For each area they examined existing social statistics, and also posed challenging questions, showing what information is needed in order to formulate policy.

There is a good deal of relevant information already available in this country, but many social scientists argue that it is not presented in any meaningful way, and it is suspected by others that, despite the general acceptance of social science techniques to identify problems, government departments fail to attach sufficient importance to the findings they are presented with.

There is a need for regular, almost continual, assessment of major government departmental policy in the light of changing social needs; and where new inventions are involved, the administrator must be able to think systematically about the economic and social consequences of the inventions, and must know what further information is required.

The new Civil Service department will have the important task of developing the study of decision theory, statistics, and management techniques as well as taking over former Treasury functions of staffing. An excellent guide to what can be done in these areas is provided by the paper produced by John Garrett and S. D. Walker[1] in which they show that setting objectives in the Civil Service requires a review of every part of the organization in terms of its contribution to the objectives as a whole. This should identify problem areas which need immediate management attention and those departments where good management exists or is absent and provide a basis for reward and promotion. Application of management-by-objectives is not an easy assignment. It requires, at all levels of management, an understanding and acceptance of the aims and methods and a willingness to accept personal accountability. In some respects this type of operational system is more easily introduced in industry or commerce, where the common aim is profitability and where there is a greater use of management control systems. Assessing the aims of the Civil Service is clearly a more complex though not impossible process. Such aims would be concerned with the legislation which a Ministry administers and with its associated functions with other departments and boards. Again, it should be possible for a department to forecast and indicate its pattern of duties and those sectors of legislation and administration in most need of change or adjustment. It is still too early to say how far the message contained in Garrett and Walker's paper is understood but it is a significant start. It is addressed to civil servants and can hardly be dodged, because the needs it emphasises are gradually being understood by politicians and they can judge, when in office or on a select committee, the extent to which these—and the Fulton proposals

[1] J. Garrett and S. D. Walker, *Management By Objectives in the Civil Service,* CAS Occasional Paper, HMSO, 1969.

—are being met. Another factor which may also highlight any failure by the Civil Service to put its house in order or any tendency to ignore the advice it has been given, is the increased use of consultants in government work.

The Civil Service organization and methods teams have also increased their activities in trying to make a more effective organization. In two years alone—1967 and 1968—their work resulted in annual savings of more than a million and a quarter pounds. Thirty-seven assignments carried out in 1967 and 1968 cost £111,725 and produced recurrent savings totalling £1,276,000 a year—eleven times their cost and double the total saved in 1965 and 1966. Further potential annual savings are estimated at £50,500.

The assignments were carried out by a Treasury O & M division that is now part of the Civil Service Department. The division gives a direct service to small and medium-sized departments and takes part in joint assignments with the O & M divisions of larger departments.

Even five years ago, savings on thirty-six assignments were assessed at £172,000. The current savings fall into three categories: direct staff savings; indirect staff savings which save time of existing staff; and savings on accommodation, storage, transport, travelling and other costs.

The following are examples of the assignments:

(i) *Land Registry:* Management review that led to a new structure.
   Result: Overall increase in productivity of 10–15 per cent (up to 40 per cent in some cases), equivalent to a saving of £600,000 a year.

(ii) *Ministry of Health:* Review of the organization and methods of the twenty-eight artificial limb and appliance centres in England and Wales, and the equivalent service in Scotland.
   Result: Savings on major recommendations £34,000 a year with a further potential £14,000.

(iii) *Home Office:* Review of the Accounts Branch.
Result: Savings of £26,000 a year.

(iv) *Home Office:* Review of the Nationality Division.
Result: Staff savings of 12½ per cent despite increased work load—worth £35,000 a year with further savings potential of £5,000 a year.

(v) *Lord Chancellor's Office:* Review of the attendant and cleaning services at the Law Courts.
Result: Savings on cleaning services of £69,000 a year with further potential savings of £13,000.

The outside management consultant has also begun to play an important role in making government more conscious of operational control and change. It is difficult to estimate the total amount which has been spent on consultancy but Kenneth Kenrick of AIC reckons on a yearly total of £4 million, if we include local government, public utilities, the armed forces and international agencies of government as well as the mainstream departments.[1] Examples of the assignments undertaken are:

(i) Studies of structure and relationships within and between departments; setting up new departments; auditing the performance of existing departments.
Examples—Fulton Report.
Management re-organization in Admiralty Dockyards in the United Kingdom.
Re-structuring the Ministry of Works in Kenya.

(ii) Regional and economic development programme.
Examples—Regional Planning studies for the South West counties of England and Wales.
Planning and development of the West Indian Sea Island Cotton industry.
London Borough of Camden—Swiss Cottage

[1] Management Consultants Association, K. Kenrick, private paper to Members of Parliament, 23 April 1969.

development—Study of desirable public and recreational amenities.
(iii) Assistance in developing marketing policies.
Examples—Studies on behalf of the National Economic Development Offices.
Marketing of new British Rail services by land and sea.
Developing recruiting campaigns for the Armed Forces.

The use of new techniques, both social science and managerial, is being introduced in the Civil Service, but the transformation will, inevitably, take time. The performance of the Civil Service, especially in regard to industry, could, however, be improved more quickly by a change in Civil Service attitudes.

The Civil Service tradition is one of great integrity and respect for intellect; in its dealings with industry a department of government must consider not only its role as sponsor of a particular industry, but also the wider implications of the national interest. In their relations with industrialists, civil servants will find themselves coping with people whose approach, because it is more single-minded, is less Olympic. The aim of the industrialist is profitability and the interests he serves are those of his own particular company; it is unreal to expect him to disclose facts which are not in that interest.

It is not suggested that civil servants should abandon their own high standards, but they should recognize that the academic approach to problems does not operate in the market-place of industrial affairs, and they must get out into that market-place and discover the facts for themselves. This may not be easy; even when the government is a shareholder in a company it cannot rely on getting all the information it requires from the company—it is not the policy of most companies to admit their shareholders to the inner workings of company finance. Nevertheless, the Civil Service must learn to probe harder, and to adopt the healthy scepticism in its approach to industry that the Industrial Reorganization Corporation has found so successful.

This means not only talking to any company that asks for
government assistance or in which the government has a financial
stake, but also talking to its competitors and knowing the state
of the industry generally, and keeping that knowledge up-to-date.
Only in this way can we avoid the kind of failure in communications which resulted in an assurance given to the House of
Commons that the Handley Page company seemed well poised
for the future being followed a few days later by the appointment
of a receiver, revealing that the company's affairs were in a
hopeless state. If government wants to be taken seriously by
industry this sort of error must be avoided, and that means that
the civil servants charged with finding the facts must be
tougher in their approach.

Government's relations with industry would be helped, too,
by a lessening in the secrecy with which the reasons for decisions
are shrouded. This springs partly from the tradition of anonymity
in the Service, a tradition which I have already suggested is
outdated. Provided only that it does not compromise the
Minister's responsibility to Parliament, there must be more
disclosure of information in this field. Otherwise, there is little
hope of getting industry to co-operate with government objectives.

One final aspect of communications in government remains to
be considered: that is, the relationship between a Minister and
his Department. It is well known that the impression made by
Ministers on their Departments varies, the variable factors being
the Minister's ability to communicate his theoretical policy, the
adaptability of the Departmental Civil Service, the amount of
time the Minister can spend with the Department, and so on.
Suggestions have already been made as to how the Civil Service
can be made more adaptable, but the process of communication
between a Minister and his Department is less susceptible to
formal changes.

The American Constitution, to some extent, obviates the difficulties presented to a Department of State by a change of
administration, by providing for some of the top departmental
positions to be Ministerial appointments. This provides the

Minister with a nucleus of like-minded men, who have the job of interpreting his policy to the Department and of supervising the overall carry-out of that policy. Some Ministries in the recent Labour Government, notably Barbara Castle, adopted a modification of this system by the appointment of "special advisers". (Labour Ministers are, in fact, more likely to encounter difficulties in communication with the Civil Service because they are less likely than the Tories to have the background found by the Fulton Social Survey of the Civil Service to be standard among civil servants.) It is a system which many more Ministers should adopt, since it would provide something nearer the most effective form of political communication described by Richard Rose, "that which requires the least amount of talk, but the greatest amount of understanding".[1]

If government is to be involved with industry, as it must, and if its actions are to be received with credibility by industry, then it is essential that government is as well equipped to cope with changes as industry, and that it is at least as well informed about particular industries as industrialists are, and has a better overall knowledge of affairs than anyone. That is what effective government is about.

[1] R. Rose, *op. cit.*

7

MAKING INDUSTRY MORE EFFICIENT

T HE INTERVENTION OF government in industrial affairs today arises mainly from the need, in a highly competitive world, to make the very best use of Britain's resources. Therefore, while some aspects of government's involvement with industry are directed towards achieving social justice, government's principal function must be to encourage industry to be more efficient—to make the best possible use of available capital, technology and manpower, at every level of its existence.

It is on this point that the whole question of government-industry relations has been brought once more into the political arena. It has been argued by Sir Keith Joseph, who must be assumed to speak for the Conservative Party leadership as a whole, that industry would become more efficient if the present tendency towards greater government involvement with industry were reversed and a series of measures introduced to encourage small business and competitive private enterprise.

This kind of approach has many pitfalls and is, to my mind, quite irrelevant to the present-day needs of industry, whether these are viewed from the industrial standpoint or that of a government charged with realising the nation's industrial potential.

To begin with, it assumes that, somewhere in the mass of small businesses, there is hidden a great deal of managerial and entrepreneurial talent, capable of responding at great speed to incentives such as changes in direct taxation and increased competition, and sparking off a new industrial revolution. There is no proof whatsoever that this is so, and such a premise is, in fact, incapable of proof, but my own experience of seven years as industrial adviser to the British Institute of Management leads me to doubt this presumption : in fact, I would go further and say that no such reservoir of talent exists. What we have to do is make the maximum use of the management talent that is already known to exist.

Even supposing that Keith Joseph is right, where is the money to float all these new enterprises going to come from? The traditional approach of the private sector suppliers of money has been to support existing businesses. They are not equipped, either in managerial talent or techniques, to change at any great rate to a policy aimed at financial growth and clamping down on static businesses. Nor is it likely that the private sector can raise the enormous sums which I have shown to be necessary for the research and development of new inventions and techniques.

In any case, competition cannot be regarded as a guarantee of efficiency. It is assumed by advocates of the *laissez-faire* approach to industry that an investment-led boom would harm only small businesses. But the experience of countries which have seen such a boom, for example, Japan and Germany, demonstrates that there are at least as many business failures as successes, and when competition is external as well as internal, the fight for existence will be harder and tougher than ever. Competition can eliminate not only the inefficient but also companies who have not yet reached their peak. Can we, as a nation, afford to waste our potential resources in cut-throat competition with each other? I submit that we cannot : we must encourage every bit of talent we have, and reserve our competitiveness for the international market-place. The home consumer can be protected equally effectively by other means.

This does not mean that the inefficient are to be coddled and feather-bedded. If it is to achieve its object of making British industry more competitive in world markets, government involvement with industry must be directed towards the elimination of waste in manpower and resources and to the encouragement of the use of modern techniques which maximise the return on both.

Use of Modern Methods

An overall strategy should be the starting point of greater

efficiency in industry and it is essential that both government and industry use the best modern methods to assist them in decision-making.

For example, one of the most important innovations in management techniques over the last decade has been DCF— Discounted Cash Flow, a method of evaluating investment decisions which, in assessing the size of cash return in relation to cash outlay, is far superior in its application to different types of projects to traditional methods of assessing investment projects. A DCF return expresses the difference between expected revenues and expected expenditures as a percentage rate of return, discounting earnings in future years to allow for the inferior value of distant returns. On this basis it is possible to assess whether the rate of return is high enough and to work out other criteria, such as market strategy.

Much work has been put into decreasing the error-proneness of DCF calculations by the Treasury and by the capital intensive part of the private sector, and four ways of dealing with this problem have been worked out. First, more effort must be put into getting the input data right, which means actually going to the trouble of working out the facts, and not relying on guess-work. Secondly, sensitivity analyses should be carried out to isolate to which variables a project's success is most sensitive. This is done by repeating the DCF calculation by feeding in variations in such things as costs, sales, market share, price, and so on, which indicates not only the difference between the worst and best results that can be expected from a particular project, but also which of many variables is the most likely to lead to failure. The isolation of significant variables is important because it enables management to make meaningful decisions about investment. The third step is a "risk analysis" which, though a time-consuming process, can quantify the effects of risks, e.g., of accepting the risk of an important variable thrown up by the "sensitivity analysis". The final step which can lead to more accurate forecasting of the results of investment is post-mortems on projects which have been in operation for some

years with the object of discovering systematic errors and errors
which could have been avoided.

"Risk analysis" in particular is a time-consuming procedure,
and is thus really only applicable to large-scale enterprises. Even
so the Treasury has recommended it to the boards of all the
nationalized industries for quantifying the effects of risk-taking.

Despite the availability of this sophisticated DCF calculation
and supporting methodology, which are widely used by top
management in the large corporations, it is doubtful whether
very many boards of directors accept DCF as the basis for their
decisions, preferring to rely on more traditional, and less reliable,
guides such as the estimate of the return on capital, or the "pay-
back period", which is based on the number of years it takes
to recover the capital cost of a product.

What can government do to ensure that industry uses the best
available techniques for deciding on its future investment projects? At the least, government should insist that these methods
are used in assessing the value of any projects in which public
money is involved. Some industrialists may be daunted by the
calculations in risk analysis, so that it is worth considering
whether it would not be worthwhile for government to provide,
on a fee-paying basis if necessary, an advisory service which
would assist a small business on the verge of enlarging its scope,
to assess the risks.

Further Rationalization Needed

The establishment of the Industrial Reorganization Corporation has gone a long way towards helping industry to restructure
and reorganize into units large enough to compete in international markets, especially with the Americans.

It is not enough to rely on the forces of the market, human,
fiscal and fashionable, to encourage mergers and take-overs, or
to provide the necessary capital for the expansion of modernization schemes. There must be some overall purpose behind restructuring and some overall benefit to be derived from it. The
IRC, which is an agency not directly responsible to government,
is in a unique position and can apply objective criteria to

structural change. It then has the necessary facilities to enable it to give effect to such restructuring as it thinks desirable. The Corporation is authorized to draw up to £150 million from public funds and from this sum it can provide loans to companies when it would be inadvisable for them to approach the commercial money market; it can allow subordination of such loans, which means that the recipients' powers to borrow elsewhere are not unduly restricted; interest payments may be deferred during the early years of a loan when rationalization costs are likely to be heavy. In addition, the Corporation is empowered to buy, sell and hold securities, form companies and give financial guarantees.

The terms and facilities are attractive and only prejudice could deny the worthiness of IRC's efforts to make industry more effective. Indeed, the fact that the Corporation fulfils a need recognized by industrialists themselves has been amply proved by the fact that the original intention of the Conservative Party to abolish the IRC if it got the opportunity has been modified under pressure from industry and they are committed only to restricting its activities.

Even this would be a mistake. The Corporation is a unique British invention, now being slavishly copied in various parts of Europe, and possibly to be imitated on a supra-national scale. It is neither a bank nor a holding company, but its record in just a few years shows what can be done to improve the international performance of manufacturing industries by promoting structural reorganization. The value of its work has already been amply demonstrated by the recent history of the computer industry.

So far, the IRC has concentrated on the task of reorganizing the manufacturing industries because therein lies the most important element in our economic life, accounting for 34 per cent of our GNP, 66 per cent of our foreign trade, and 34 per cent of our working population. But the Managing Director of the Corporation, Charles Villiers, has an even more adventurous approach to the IRC, with a grand design for a European IRC which could "promote, assist and accelerate the restructuring of industry between European companies". The IRC already has government permission to raise money in European markets and use it for promoting Anglo-European co-operation on industrial projects, a theme to which I shall return later.

In fact, one proposed industrial merger has already anticipated any action of the IRC in Europe, as well as Britain's hoped-for entry into the European Economic Community : that is, the proposed association between Dunlop and Pirelli. Although there is much work to be done before the merger becomes a fact—the proposals have to be accepted by the shareholders, the British and Italian Governments and the Common Market Commission—it is a logical move which will lead to economies in the setting up of a string of plants round the world and give the combined companies bargaining power in their relations with their largest customer, the motor giants.

At present Dunlop has 128 factories and Pirelli 82, employing respectively, 102,500 and 76,000 throughout the world. The combined groups would be the fifty-fourth largest in the world, the fifteenth largest outside the United States, and the third largest tyre manufacturers in the world. The intention is for each group to take a substantial share, in the region of 40 to 49 per cent, in the activities of the other.

What factors have led to this proposed merger? Some of them may apply only to the specific industry, but the general trends are relevant to industry in general. The two companies already co-operate to a very large extent because of the nature of the industry. The biggest market for motor tyres is the replacement market, but this is largely influenced by the tyres put on the car by the manufacturer. There is therefore strong competition for original equipment contracts, at prices which often show little or no profit, and, as the world trade in vehicles has grown, tyre manufacturers have found it necessary to open plants in more and more markets, both to capture replacement sales for exported vehicles and to supply original tyres to overseas assembly plants. Another factor in local manufacture rather than direct export is the local content in motor manufacture which most developing countries demand from local subsidiaries of international firms.

The entry of the Japanese into the race for world motor markets has increased still further the rate at which motor manufacturers are setting up overseas assembly plants and, because of the establishment of a European technical lead in the development of radial cord tyres (relevant to this particular merger, as Dunlop make their radial tyres to Pirelli patents, but Dunlop has a lead in the more detailed know-how about the design of such tyres) the European tyre industry sees a chance of winning for the first time a significant share of the American market. The proposed Dunlop-Pirelli merger gives Pirelli access to the whole English-speaking world, as Dunlop has big markets in North America and the Commonwealth as well as Northern Europe, while Pirelli, as the most international of the European companies, has large outlets in Southern Europe and Latin America.

The Dunlop-Pirelli story shows the factors which our manufacturing industries are continually meeting in their sorties into international markets. Their main competitors for developing markets are the Americans, whose technology-based industries have the advantage of an enormous home market to serve as a jumping-off point for the export markets. The British home market cannot be expanded much further and it is therefore necessary to expand our overseas markets; this is true not only for this country but for all the Western European countries. The case of Dunlop and Pirelli demonstrates that industry realizes the need for European integration even where governments are slow to bring this about.

To return, however, to the British industrial scene, the question is whether IRC can make many inroads into the restructuring of industry on its own. Of course it cannot. But the State provides a wide range of services to further its objectives (see Appendix I). And there is another factor to be taken into account when we are considering the merging of industrial units and that is the role of the Board of Trade. The Board is inevitably anxious to satisfy economic and industrial as well as social interests. Until recently it had the responsibility of showing whether a proposed merger was permissible under existing legislation and of producing within a reasonably short time, a report on any doubts which might exist on the probable consequences of such a merger. The Board's researches covered the companies involved (their operating figures, turnover, breakdown of turnover by product); the industry or market (the range of products affected by the merger and the structure of the industry); and the merger proposal (the stated motives of the firms concerned, the firm's intention and factories to be closed).

A guide to the work load is shown in the number and value of mergers considered by the Board and those referred to the Monopolies Commission.

TABLE I

Number and Value of Mergers considered by Board of Trade

	1965	1966	1967	1968					Cumulative Total 1965–1968
	TOTAL	TOTAL	TOTAL	1	2	3	4	TOTAL	
Number	48	58	93	39	25	27	28	119	318*
Gross Assets (£m).	431	566	869	283	287	715	707	1,992	3,858

* In addition there were 23 proposed newspaper mergers, 12 banking and 12 building society mergers, making a grand total of 365 by the end of 1968. On 30th June, 1969, the grand total stood at 430. The banking and building society cases have been omitted from Table 1 because they would have greatly distorted the assets figures; and the newspapers because the Act provides special procedures for them.

The table shows the rapid increase in the number and scale of the mergers. The figures, it should be noted, relate to *proposed* mergers considered by the Board, and do not correspond to *actual* mergers completed in the same period.

Of the twelve mergers listed, eight were found by the Commission not to be contrary to the public interest (including the two newspaper mergers). In three cases the Commission concluded that the mergers would operate against the public interest (Nos. 2, 7 and 12) and in a fourth case (No. 10), the Commission recommended by a narrow majority that it would be contrary to the public interest but it was too divided to constitute a formal recommendation.

TABLE 2
Mergers referred to the Monopolies Commission

A summary of mergers recommended for reference to the Commission since the 1965 Act is given below.

		Mergers referred	*Time allowed (Months)*	*Time taken (Months)*
1965	1.	B.M.C./Pressed Steel	6	3
1966	2.	Ross Group and Associated Fisheries	3	3
	3. (a)	The Dental Manufacturing Co. and the Amalgamated Dental Co.	6	5
	3. (b)	The Dentists Supply Co. and the A.D.C.		
	4.	GKN/Birfield	6	5
	5.	B.I.C.C./Pyrotenax	6	4½
	6.	Times/Sunday Times	3	2½
1967	7.	United Drapery Stores and Montague Burton	4	3
	8.	Thomson Newspapers/Crusha	3	2½
1968	9.	Thorn Electrical and Radio Rentals	4	under 4
	10.	Barclays/Lloyds/Martins	6	5
1969	11.	Unilever/Allied Breweries	4	under 4
	12.	Rank Organisation/De La Rue	4	under 4

The work of the Monopolies Commission has, in some cases, notably brewing and certain professional services, overlapped with the work of the National Board for Prices and Incomes. The Labour government was proposing to merge the two bodies into the Commission for Industry and Manpower, under the aegis of the Department of Employment and Productivity, who have already taken over responsibility for the two bodies and will in future also watch over the work of the Restrictive Practices Court.

The theory behind the re-alignment was that the new body, which would do the same sort of work as its predecessors, with some new functions, would be able to police the consequences of mergers more thoroughly, and would also be able to take a more active role in preventing abuses of market power, especially cases where apparently fierce competition among companies masks activities which are contrary to the public interest. Besides responsibility for monopolies, mergers and major concerns, the CIM would have far-ranging powers to investigate selected wage and price movements which, in the hands of a strong Chairman, could extend into much wider examinations of company efficiency.

The final structure of the CIM was awaiting the outcome of discussions between the Department of Employment and Productivity, the Confederation of British Industry and the Trades Union Congress at the time of the 1970 Election. Its future is now in doubt and it is already known that the CBI are opposed to the sponsoring of the new board by the DEP.

Whether the CIM would prove strong enough to carry out its policing activities efficiently is a debatable point. The DEP is already the subject of criticism for its failure to make strong enough references to the PIB and the Monopolies Commission had powers, such as the power of reversing mergers, which were never used. The civil servants from the Board of Trade's Monopolies and Mergers section will, it is true, supply some new talent to the DEP, but despite the interest and activity they have shown so far in their tackling of mergers, they have not yet developed a consistent approach.

The main requirement is a strong Chairman with a senior trade unionist as his deputy. The new Commission is potentially a very valuable tool in the government's plans to increase industrial efficiency.

Management and Industrial Efficiency

The ways in which modern management techniques should be applied to the running of government have already been suggested. But it would be a mistake to assume that the existence of these techniques means that they are as widely used as they could be throughout industry.

It is not difficult to find evidence that much of the responsibility for inferior performance by British industry can be laid at the door of British management. One of the most important studies in this field is Professor John H. Dunning's comparative study of the performance of US subsidiaries in Britain and their UK competitors.[1] Professor Dunning demonstrates that American

[1]*Business Ratios,* No. 1 (Autumn 1966) pp. 5–18.

subsidiaries in Britain earn substantially higher after-tax profits on net assets than British public companies, and that over the period from 1950–64, the American figures exceeded the UK ones by 77 per cent. The study shows that no factors of the nature of, for example, different accounting procedures, can be held to explain the difference, and Professor Dunning is able to produce calculations which show the nature of American managerial superiority : American firms have a lower ratio of administration to direct costs, higher labour productivity and greater capital/labour intensity.

The Professor concludes that there is some reason to suppose that the higher profits earned by American firms are due at least partly to the greater amount of research and managerial knowledge available to them and to the better formal qualifications of their executives, with factors such as labour turnover and labour relations playing only a very limited role. What adds weight to his findings is his study of the influence of US parent companies on local decision-taking; while the statistics he produces are not conclusive either way, wholly owned US subsidiaries record higher profits than jointly financed companies, and those with American Managing Directors seem to do considerably better than those with UK Managing Directors. The optimum degree of American control seems to vary from department to department—marketing policy seems best when American methods are slightly modified and capital expenditure and industrial relations seem to be best handled on a local level, but it is clear that the American contribution to management expenditure is very significant.

The management gap between Britain—indeed the whole of Western Europe—and the United States (and the USSR) lies very largely in the failure of this country to educate its managers for the job. The cult of amateurism, which has so bedevilled the Civil Service, has also served to hold back industrial management, and nepotism has added to the problems. This is probably less true now than it was ten years ago, but it is still a field in which much remains to be done.

The education gap exists through the whole field of higher

and adult education and can to some extent be traced back
even as far as primary education which, by premature streaming
prevents the full development of a child's potential. The relaxation in the streaming system and the development of comprehensive education will, it is hoped, play their part in improving
the quality of future entrants to industry. But the British system
is still geared to the idea of education as a once-for-all process
rather than the permanent process it is held to be under the
American system. The American system is more flexible, allowing for a wider range of higher education courses, late entry and
learning at any age.

So far as higher education is concerned, a statistical comparison of the United States with Western Europe, represented
by Great Britain, France, Germany and Italy, shows that
American expenditure on education was 6.5 of the GNP as
against 4.2 for Europe, and that enrolment for higher education
in 1966, for example, was 30 per 1,000 heads of population as
against 6.5 per 1,000 for Europe. Added to this, 15 per cent of
public and private college students are enrolled in the 600
business schools in the United States, which means that young
graduates are much more economically orientated than their
European counterparts.

There is, therefore, a great need for specialized training in
management and related techniques in this country. Fortunately
the whole approach to industrial training, including management
training, has become much more professional in the last few
years. There are now some twenty-six industrial training boards
in existence, as well as nearly 500 group training schemes,
covering every aspect of industrial training from the apprenticeship of school leavers to the training of management, under the
direction of the Central Training Council. They cover a wide
range of basic and manufacturing industries, public utilities,
transport and service industries, employing some fifteen million
workers, about 85 per cent of the total numbers who fall within
the scope of the Industrial Training Acts.

It is not only the quantity of training available which has
increased; there has also been a considerable improvement in

quality. The training boards have a wide measure of autonomy and are backed by the work of the Central Training Council and the joint committee boards to secure some identity of approach to occupations common to more than one industry. The close relationship between training and vocational education in its widest sense has been taken into account, resulting in voluntary co-operation between the training boards and the education authorities who are responsible for the provision of further education generally.

The work of the Central Training Council and of the training boards on management is of particular importance. It has, at last, been realized that the continuous improvement of standards of management is critical to the well-being of the whole economy, and is especially important because ultimate responsibility for all forms of training rests with management.

There have been many pronouncements suggesting that the way to improve the quality of management education is to promote more courses. In fact, I am convinced that what is needed most is *qualitative* improvement.

Part of the difficulty of establishing the importance of management development and education is the inability of senior management to understand the changing role of the manager and the use of systematic method. It may appear that there is a close relationship between the nature of the problem in government and industry. But I would argue that the need for improvement is likely to be more acute in industry because the gap between the progressive firms and those operating in a narrow and outdated framework is always widening.

The new role of the manager in industry involves him increasingly in establishing firm objectives and in the making of plans to achieve them. For, whilst one hesitates to call management a science, there are undoubtedly theories which could be said to form a management concept, which managers should know about, and this concept is dynamic and flexible: dynamic, as research and accumulated experience lead to a greater understanding, and flexible, because of the unpredictability of human nature which prevents the adoption of a stock response to every situation.

The much-debated question of whether management is a science or an art has always been irrelevant. In the preparation of evidence, however, management could be said to be a science, using scientific methods and tools. Has the knowledge and use of these and related techniques helped the manager to develop a more professional outlook in his job? Managers have clearly emerged over the last half century as a distinct group and during recent years their function has been seen to be quite specific. In terms of decision-making, medium and large-scale industry is predominantly controlled by managers, rather than by owners but this trend has not always been accompanied by an equivalent development in professionalism. The solution to this discrepancy lies in the involvement of senior management in training. In Britain, executives have not exposed themselves to training to the degree that they have in the United States nor indeed to the extent of their own juniors, or employees of operative level whose training is of a very high standard. A training programme must be closely integrated with company policy if it is not to develop spasmodically and this demands that the training specialist be placed in the management team.

Continued progress in management training is the Department of Employment and Productivity's major training objective. The Central Training Council has produced two reports on management and supervisory training. Both emphasize six basic requirements for adequate management training schemes: the assignment of responsibility to a senior member of the firm; analysis of managerial jobs; appraisal of performance and potential; assessment of the firm's present and future needs for managers; keeping of records; and construction of training programmes. For training to develop successfully within a company—and this is particularly true of management training—it is essential that directors and senior management help to create a climate in which such schemes can develop. It is essential for one senior manager in every company to take responsibility for management training, and for that individual to keep in touch himself

with the training board, expressing the view of the training
board to his colleagues, and expressing the views of his company
to the training board.

Good and effective management training and development
cannot be over-estimated in its contribution towards meeting
the objectives of the organization, whether it is industry or
government. The new management processes demand new
attitudes as much as new systems. The scientific tools mentioned
are available to management and these mark the beginning of
a new professionalism in management. It is towards these that
industry has to direct its attention if it wants to get the most out
of its human resources. Much has been written about the
technical, modern systematic methods, like operational research
and budgeting control but there are others, involving the improvement of human effectiveness, which have received less
attention.

(i) *Interfirm Comparison*

Interfirm comparisons provide management with some key
statistics to show how a firm's operating performance and
financial results compare with those of similar firms in the
same industry or trade, after their figures have been pooled.
Comparisons help managers by revealing weaknesses in their
businesses which need remedying before competitive standards
of performances can be reached; and by suggesting the lines
on which such improvements should be made. Many thousands of firms in this country and abroad have already had
practical proof of the value of this systematic pooling and
interpretation of statistics.

(ii) *Labour-turnover Analysis*

It has long been established that a high rate of labour
turnover leads to inefficiency and adds to production costs.
By systematically analysing the reasons for "separations" and
by breaking down the cost of replacements it is possible both
to find why and where wastage occurs and to work out labour-
turnover budgets. For instance, the background causes of
labour-turnover were studied in forty South Wales companies

(Lloyd,[1] 1958) and a subsequent analysis of all the causes produced valuable evidence relating to selection and training, which could not otherwise have come to light.

(iii) *Selection, Appraisal, Training*

Stocktaking is a normal process in most organizations and is valuable when applied to personnel and development policies as well as to materials and products. With a management inventory, the obvious questions which arise are : What is the average age of senior management? Which senior manager is due to retire in five years; in ten years? A similar appraisal of middle and junior management may be made. Further questions which may be asked are : What part of the management team have university degrees? What is the general educational level of the team? This basic assessment of management material is frequently omitted in many businesses. Stocks amass or deteriorate with no thought of possible supply and demand in the future.

When management policy is as haphazard as this, we get the deformity known as "crisis management", grotesque and incalculable. All undertakings should adopt regular scientific assessments of the management position. It is essential to :

(*a*) Review the present management team, and note its effectiveness and shortcomings.

(*b*) Help those likely to benefit from training or special skills courses, and consider those who have neither the intellectual capacity to develop nor the desire to take responsibility which a senior post demands.

(*c*) Recruit new staff when necessary.

Full job descriptions need to be used in the recruitment of staff which will arise from a management or staff inventory. The practice of some companies, which tell the candidate that his career will be worked out as he progresses, is pernicious. The components of the job should be described; the flexible element

[1]Lloyd, *Report based on a survey of labour turnover in the administrative county of Monmouthshire,* Monmouth Technical College, 1958.

which will, of course, depend on the interests and ability of the applicant should be emphasized. Then the type of candidate required should be specified according to qualifications and experience.

Knowledge and use of these techniques will not only help industrial management in its own establishments but it will also contribute to stimulating a dialogue with those who serve government.

A New Employee Information System

If maximum government and all external information is to be made there is a very real need for an improved communication system within our firms. An imaginative approach is required, so that employees are not isolated from the decision-making process themselves. In many firms known to me the standard and performance of management has improved as a result of employee pressure initially requesting information and consultative meetings. While there can be no substitute for effective executive action, there are sectors of decision-making which can be examined and assessed if not shared by employees.

The main aim of employee information systems must be a single channel of representation. This would remove the structure set up to maintain the false distinction between subjects for bargaining and those considered appropriate for consultation. Employee participation needs to be closely linked with trade union organization. The government should guarantee by legislation the right of employees to organize and secure recognition; it must ensure the provision to employee representatives of increased information on the firm and its behaviour, on the development of industry, and the economy, within which participation would be virtually impossible. Practical aid to the workshop representative would be required to back up such measures; for instance, time off to do union work, and reimbursement for loss of earnings; training facilities and release to take advantage of them; office facilities; access to members and facilities for conducting ballots and holding meetings.

The type of information which management would be expected to pass on would include :

(i) *Manpower and Remuneration Questions*

Labour force; labour turnover; manpower plan and staff development; absenteeism and sickness rates; accident rates and trends; accident prevention plans including training; other training schemes; labour costs per unit of output; payroll details and methods of payments; managerial and directorial emoluments; and qualifications of directors and senior management.

(ii) *Control Questions*

Details concerning holding, subsidiary, and associated companies; directors' shareholdings in the company; beneficial control of nominee shareholdings; internal management structure and definition of decision-making responsibilities.

(iii) *Development, Production, and Investment Questions*

Proposed changes of a substantial character in methods of work and/or labour requirements; state of the order book and trend of orders gained and lost; research, development, and investment plans; purchasing policies.

(iv) *Cost, Pricing and Profit Questions*

Cost and pricing structures; breakdown by plant or product where applicable; turnover; financing of development.

The dissemination of some of the information specified here would mean further legislation. A start has been made on this with the 1966 Companies Act. If efficiency is to be examined it must be possible to measure it and compare, for instance, the strong sectors and the weaknesses in an industry with other industries and other nations; only in this way is it possible to assess standards of performance, and provide management and representatives of the operational staffs with a method for testing their own achievements.

The 1970s are likely to produce even more changes in the industrial environment and make even greater demands on management than did the 1960s. The change will come partly from the fact that management is now recognized as a technique, about which we are learning more and more every day. Another factor, which is already beginning to reveal itself, is the change in attitudes between the generations, between those who bore the task of management through the inter-war years of depression and through the strains of wartime and those who are rising to the top as the first-fruits of the 1944 Education Act and the climate that produced it, the new "meritocracy". The third important factor will be the one which has, to a large extent, dominated the theme of this book, the pressures of international competition and the wider markets. It is essential that management is able to absorb new concepts intellectually and to translate them into action; for this purpose management training needs to be a continuous process, with adequate opportunities for those in the higher echelons of management to acquire new techniques as they become available. Among the most important of these techniques are those of communication.

I think it is difficult to over-estimate the importance of communication in industry, in government, or in any other field. Good communication is the essence of sound industrial relations and must therefore be regarded as the first essential of training. As a process taking place within industry, communication has been the subject of study and definition by sociologists, psychologists, and experts in organisational theory, and it is therefore reasonable to expect that a proper understanding of the subject and practical suggestions as to the ways in which barriers to communication can be overcome would lie in an approach which brought together all these areas of expertise.

The study of psychology is widely used in industry for a number of purposes, for example, in the fields of selection, appraisal, attitude surveys and communications generally. Every work situation involves some degree of communication between one person and another: sometimes this is direct and simple; in other situations it can be a complicated pattern of messages and responses to them. The manager's particular responsibility for communications arises from the variation in response which the same message induces according to who receives it.

A manager cannot be trained to communicate in such a way as to eliminate entirely any possibility of misunderstanding. Yet, psychological training is important because it brings about understanding of the relevance of such things as personal background and experience (which might all seem irrelevant) as well as obvious factors such as the work environment, the processes of information and advice and the kind of response which particular approaches are likely to call forth.

A knowledge of sociology is important, too. A manager who fails to appreciate the nature of social change since the end of the last century is unlikely to understand such things as what holds a work group together and what gives it satisfaction. Working people are now better-educated, better-organized, and more powerful economically than ever before. The old boss/worker relationship is no longer relevant, and the system that supported it, by which orders were issued and obeyed without question, without anyone caring whether or not they were understood, has crumbled. Workers now want, and are capable of, a share in the running of industry.

Industrial society, like society generally, consists of a number of groups which are constantly changing. A manager whose training includes some sociology will understand that these groups have a life of their own and will use his knowledge of their varying influence to ensure that all the groups within his responsibility work in harmony and not in conflict with one another. It is not enough to know simply the laid-down structure of a company; who has authority and who has not. A manager must also be aware of any less formal powers-that-be. Good communications have been shown by a number of studies to occur most frequently in firms where the organization structure is clearly defined. But in all organizations there will also be a secondary structure arising from, for example, men working in the same trade in different departments meeting together to discuss common problems.

The communication process is complicated by all these factors and becomes more complex as the size of the organization increases, especially when the expansion arises from a merger or take-over, when other structures, equally complicated, have to be accommodated. Such changes as this, and any major change brought about by the application of new technology, may demand an entirely new approach to the flow of information within a company.

In short: communication is the passing on of feelings and ideas by an individual or group to another individual or group, and where necessary, the obtaining of an informed response.

The heaviest responsibility for ensuring that communication fulfils all its purposes lies with the individual manager. Communication is a central activity of industrial leadership and training; it is at the grass-roots of industrial relations.

The techniques of communication can, fortunately, be learned. They should be included in all training schemes, and large organizations should carry out internal surveys to discover whether their communications procedures work satisfactorily.[1]

Taxation and Incentives

It is often argued, especially by employers' and industrialists' organizations such as the CBI, and more recently by the Conservative Party spokesman, Sir Keith Joseph, that industry could be made to function more effectively by the use of taxation incentives to investment. Such incentives do, to some extent, already exist in the shape of tax relief: there is a capital allowance which permits the deduction from profits of up to all the cost of new plant and equipment or capital works carried out, and an allowance is made for depreciation either on a percentage basis throughout the whole period of use, or until the amount of depreciation allowance reaches the capital cost. In addition, industries in development areas get relief at a higher rate, through the system of investment allowances.

But investment by itself does not solve the problem of increasing industrial growth if inefficient techniques are used to decide where investment should be applied and inadequate management fails to maximise the return on investment. The

[1]See, for an expansion of this topic, Eric Moonman, *Communication in an Expanding Organization*, Tavistock, 1970.

main function of taxation in the industrial area must, therefore, be the encouragement of economic efficiency. SET, although an unpopular tax which has not entirely achieved its purpose of making industry less labour-intensive by encouraging the use of larger quantities of other production factors in conjunction with labour, nevertheless, is on the right lines. In particular, the rebating of tax to manufacturing industries, thereby encouraging manufacturing and, indirectly, exports, is an idea which could, perhaps, be more widely used to encourage other desirable tendencies.

Public Ownership

Nationalization has always been regarded as a political and specifically socialist approach to the relationship of government and industry. What has often been overlooked is that most of the industries which have been nationalized are those which have failed at some level to meet public demand for the services which the industry existed to supply, either because of failure to realize the nature of the demand or because the state of industrial relations in the industry made efficient functioning impossible (e.g. the coal industry and the docks).

The question of efficiency in industry arises in two ways in connection with public ownership : first, in government's responsibility for the existing nationalized industries, and secondly, in deciding whether or not nationalization is an appropriate tool for government to use in making a particular industry more efficient.

Government control of the nationalized industries has been under review recently by the Select Committee on Nationalized Industries, which has analysed the institutions and procedures within and through which ministerial control is currently exercised in order to determine the success of government departmental control. The Committee attempted, in its long overdue review, to determine whether the limits of ministerial control should be defined by statute, by the adoption of economic and administrative principles and rules, or by informal arrangements and undertakings between Ministers and Boards.

The Committee's suggestions as to the guiding principles for the efficient operation of nationalized industries within a framework of social and economic requirements are particularly relevant to this study. It was suggested that the responsible Ministers should continue to ensure the efficiency of the industries by exercising a broad oversight of them, but that they should not become involved in actual management; in other words, ministerial control should be strategical rather than tactical. The Committee also recommended that there should be a clear demarcation of responsibilities both between government departments and between Ministers and Boards. Their final recommendation was that both the Ministers and the industries should be publicly accountable. Responsibilities for actions, successes and failures, should be publicly identifiable. Ministers should be accountable to Parliament both for themselves and for the industries, and the Boards, when necessary, should also be accountable to Parliament. In other words, the Committee suggests a considerable change from the traditional role of government as controller or intervenor in the nationalised industries to one of adviser or sponsor.

The major weakness of the existing structure is the underlying confusion of responsibilities between the sponsoring Departments. For example, what are the respective responsibilities of the Treasury and the sponsoring Departments for the investment programme and what are the responsibilities of Ministers in relation to staff and wages questions? Ambiguities of this kind have led, at the very least, to considerable duplication of effort, and could equally well produce total inaction.

The Committee's recommendation of a Minister for Nationalized Industries implies the need to separate those operations which are managerial in character and those which have a political content. Certainly the Committee's conclusions suggest possibilities of structural reorganization which might easily apply to other government Departments, both in their relations with private industry directly and in the implementation of their own programmes. For example, the Health Service might be run by managers (on principles and methods of industrial efficiency) and guide lines might be laid down by the Ministry of Health.

The transfer of the functions of the Ministry of Power to the Ministry of Technology has gone some way towards implementing this latter decision, and in some ways is an even more logical approach. Mintech's function is now that of sponsorship of industry in general, and there is possibly more inclination to apply the same criteria of efficiency to the nationalized industries as to those in the private sector than would be the case if there were a separate Ministry which controlled social services such as the Health Service and the various fuel and power industries.

The question of whether nationalization is an appropriate method of reviving a failing industry is a more difficult one. For one thing, it is no longer the only way in which government can acquire a stake in an industry into which it has injected public money. I would suggest that the cases where it is most appropriate are those where no other solution is feasible, that is, where the industry, though still necessary to the country, has virtually broken down completely. And if nationalization is felt to be the solution to an industry's problems, we must learn from past mistakes. In particular, nationalization must be seen as a new beginning: taking over the management which has failed to run an industry efficiently in the past is not the way to ensure it a prosperous future.

Where a "rescue operation" is less radical, there are other, more appropriate ways for government to see the finance it puts into an industry is used in the public interest; for example, the acquisition of a share in the company's equity. Once again, a good example of how this can be done is the case study on the computer industry.

There is also the new type of public corporation, exemplified by the proposed corporations for the manufacture and sale of atomic fuels and radio isotopes, which are able to raise money in the public market. This one is especially applicable to the question of making the results of government scientific research commercially viable. Joint ventures with the private sector are

another way in which government can stimulate growth, especially in international markets. British Petroleum has led the way
here in its breakthrough into the American market, but smaller
undertakings, such as the National Coal Board's ventures with
appliance manufacturers and the like, have also achieved some
success.

The Trade Unions

What is the role of the trade unions in the partnership
between government and industry? What can governments do
to encourage the existence of good relations?

Part of the difficulty has always been in the negative attitude
of the trades unions to these questions. It is not so much that
they have failed to work out a satisfactory role in their relationships with government and the employers, but that they, with
some exceptions, have never properly appreciated the dynamics
of change amongst their own membership. To put it another
way: British trade unions as represented by large numbers of
their officers have failed to make changes in their functions which
would go some way towards meeting the contemporary requirements of their membership, both social and psychological. Of
course, the trade unions still have a protectionist function to perform and always will whilst companies like Roberts Arundel in
Stockport are around. Of course, they have to take employers to
task when shoddy work practices are perpetuated. But I would
argue strongly that the "raison d'etre" of the modern trade union
involves more than the taking of defensive action.

Successive TUC conferences have called for a new approach
but where is it to be found? Where are the experiments in communication amongst union members being carried out? After
all, if branch meetings are habitually badly attended, someone in
the TUC and at union headquarters should be interested. It is a
condemnation of trade union progress that one can find references to industrial democracy made at trade union conferences
a hundred years ago yet there is still no evidence of a practical
application today. What action, for instance, have trade union
research workers, of which there are now more than fifty, taken

on that fine analysis of works communication systems by Professor Eric Rhenman (*Industrial Democracy*) published last year? From my own enquiries and observations I regret to say that few have even heard of it.

It is quite clear that the trade unions have a positive role to play in the partnership between government and employers but it is taking them a long time to come off the defensive. The governments—particularly Tory governments—are not going to help them in their dilemma. It may be that a Tory Minister at the DEP will charm the unions with a smooth line initially, but fundamentally, the Conservatives are committed to a legalistic solution to the problem of industrial discontent. Obviously this shows a lack of understanding of what industrial unrest is about. The assumption is that "strikes" are phenomena with a life, an origin of their own: it ignores the fact that strikes are usually symptomatic of deep-seated grievances, failures in general industrial relations, as well and as much as protests against cold tea or the obscene language of a new foreman.

Unfortunately, neither the measured conclusions of the Royal Commission nor the struggles of the Labour government over the penal clauses have yet convinced the Conservative Party of the irrelevance in the industrial context of legalistic solutions, and, the 1970 election having brought a change of government, the whole matter will have to be gone through again, to the detriment of industry at large. Some idea of the type of solution which the Conservative leadership finds attractive can be found in the evidence given to the Donovan Commission by the Inns of Court Conservative and Unionist Society. Their two main proposals are the appointment of a Registrar, with wide powers of inspection and control, and the establishment of regional industrial courts under a national industrial court, with a right of appeal in certain cases to the House of Lords.

The Registrar would maintain a register of trade unions and employers' associations. Those bodies on the register would enjoy certain privileges not available to unregistered bodies, and the Registrar would have wide discretion in approving union constitutions and organization, subject to the supervision of the proposed industrial courts.

These, besides exercising this supervisory jurisdiction over the Registrar, would consider complaints by employees against unjust dismissals, consider refusals to admit to trade unions, consider complaints about disciplinary action by the unions, adjudicate on disputes where both parties are agreed on such a reference to the courts, and, most important of all in the eyes of the Conservative lawyers, adjudicate on breaches of collective agreements to which either an employers' association or a trade union is a party: the Conservative Party is anxious to give the force of law to such agreements, envisaging the award of damages as the remedy for a breach. The damages, to which a limit is proposed, would be recoverable from a union, which would in its turn be able to recover from the members concerned in the breach.

These proposals came from the Conservative lawyers and not from the Party spokesman, but the events of the early months of 1970, notably the Selsdon Park conference of Tory leaders, has made it abundantly clear that the Conservative Party has every intention of "taking on" the trade unions, and that the centrepiece of their proposals is a legally binding contract. Legislation would put an agreement between an employer and a union on a par with a commercial contract, binding on both sides. Such an agreement would include procedures for settling disputes, and, if these were ignored by unofficial strikers, the men could be sued for damages.

The adoption of these proposals would, I am convinced, far from preventing industrial disruption, almost certainly lead to industrial chaos. First, because the processes of the industrial courts would be a cumbersome and slow method of reaching agreement in an industrial dispute, and it is accepted by anyone with experience in this field that speed is essential when a dispute is to be resolved without leaving scars, if not running sores, on the industrial body politic. Secondly, the initiation of innumerable actions for petty debt, as the unions try to recover damages from their members, would exacerbate relations between a union and its members, consume the unions' time and money to no purpose, striking at the root of the unions' good health. That this would please the employers no more than the unions was made clear by the Chairman of the Birmingham Chamber of Commerce in a recent speech in which he warned that any legislation that drove a wedge between the unions and the rank and file employees could do nothing but harm. At present it is possible to rely on agreements with the unions having some effect, but if the unions are forced into a position where they are distrusted by their members, such agreements will not be worth the bother of making them.

The contract system also contains one major loophole which, even if other factors did not operate, would make it an unsatisfactory means to industrial peace. A commercial contract is only legally binding if both sides agree that it should be; either side can opt out of legal liability by insisting on the insertion of a clause stating that the contract should not be enforceable in the courts. The Transport and General Workers' Union already has a policy which prevents its officials from signing agreements containing penalty clauses, and their example is likely to be followed by other unions. So, whether the Conservative approach is viewed from the standpoint of legal enforceability or the more important human relations view, proposals of this nature are seen as irrelevant to the human relations problems which lie at the root of most industrial disputes.

The point has now, it seems, been taken to heart by the Labour Party, and solutions are being sought to the problems of industrial unrest in other directions, notably the Commission on Industrial Relations already mentioned and in the new powers which the TUC has taken on itself to intervene in inter-union disputes and in disputes between unions and their members. It seems likely that one factor in the prevalence of unofficial strikes is a loss of confidence by the rank and file in union leadership, which is felt to be too remote from the problems involved. One answer to this, and one which seems to show an understanding of the realities of industrial life, was suggested by Mrs. Castle in a speech to the Industrial Society

New Action group on 22 October 1969, when she said that management must recognize that the unions will have to give shop stewards an increasingly important role. "It means that negotiations are increasingly going to take place with shop floor representatives and that industrial action will be endemic unless management conducts its part of the agreement much more effectively and at the real point of negotiation (the shop floor) rather than in the boardroom."

One thing is clear: we must look for human solutions to the problems of industrial strife.

What is needed, in fact, is a realisation of the idea of industrial democracy, in which workers have a full understanding of and a real stake in the industries for which they work.

The unions must lose their traditionally cautious approach to new ideas and begin by introducing more actively democratic procedures within their own organization, so that the role of the shop stewards is integrated into the structure as a whole. This alone would reduce the risk of "wildcat" as opposed to official strikes. There has been a breakdown in the lines of communication and control in the organizational pyramid, which has meant that some union leadership is completely out of touch with the rank and file, whose views are only made known by local action and unofficial strikes.

The main problem, therefore, is one of communications, already shown to be an essential tool of management. The solutions to the unions' problems of communication are similar. First, the respective roles of shop stewards and union officials must be clearly defined in union rule books and shop stewards' handbooks, and the extent of their power to negotiate locally must be made clear and a relevant procedure defined. But the defining of functions must also be accompanied by changes in the structure and administration of the unions. For example, where numbers permit, unions should base their branches on particular plants, to encourage participation by non-active members and to strengthen the link between the shop stewards and the branch officials, who are responsible for two-way communication between the shop floor and the union leadership.

Historical and industrial circumstances may influence the degree to which this kind of branch organization operates, but in industries with a high incidence of failure of communication between shop floor and union this would be a fairly simple way of improving things.

Other possibilities relate to an increase in the number of full-time officials, the recognition by the unions of joint committees of shop stewards in plants where several unions are engaged, and adequate publicity and attention to the rules for all elections, however lowly the union post involved, to prevent take-over by irresponsible or subversive elements.

The most important measure, however, is the strengthening of the union administrative machine. This means better educational facilities, better research facilities, and better salaries for top officials, so that the quality of staff is good. If the unions are to play their part in national economic planning and the introduction of new technologies, more education is needed to generate an understanding among all union members, right down to shop-floor level, of the policies of the union. In particular, it is important that shop stewards are endowed with greater knowledge and skill for the fulfilment of their task in industry. All unions should have an educational staff, and the meagre 2 per cent of union income commonly devoted to educational purposes must be increased to a more realistic level.

The Commission on Industrial Relations has an important part to play. So far, it has been concerned only with reporting and recommending solutions for individual industries with a particularly bad record in industrial relations, and it has been slow to act because it must be asked to do so by the Department of Employment and Productivity, who carry out a preliminary inquiry themselves. These individual case studies are, of course, valuable, especially when, like the Birmingham Metal Industries report, they make clear the fact that industrial unrest is a state of mind, to which many factors contribute, and not the result of one particular incident. But the CIR should not be restricted to specific inquiries: the whole field of industrial relations should be open to its scrutiny, and it should be able to recommend action to unions as well as to management about questions of structure and communications.

Industrial democracy must be made a reality by making decision-making at all levels of industrial organization a shared process. Besides job satisfaction, status in the working community, and good personal relations, workers should also have some degree of control in matters that are directly related to pay and conditions of work and rewards generally; they should have an obligation to assist in the analysis which management makes from time to time of positive features in the working environment as well as failures; and workers must be able to put forward detailed proposals and take the initiative in introducing items of policy that are less controversial but which affect all workers, such as welfare facilities and refreshment arrangements.

Workers' councils or committees are a feature of industrial life in a number of countries, notably Israel, Sweden, Western Germany, and Yugoslavia; their actual organization varies according to the political systems and the development of social and economic forces in the countries concerned, but there can be little doubt of their value in promoting good industrial relations. This is another area which the Commission on Industrial Relations could well examine.

One aspect of industrial democracy which has been much discussed is the question of how workers can be given a stake in the capital of the industry. Various measures have been proposed—nationalization was thought of as one answer, but it is doubtful whether many employees of the railways, for example, think of themselves as having any more stake in their industry than do employees of Marks and Spencers. Nor do I think that co-ownership and profit-sharing are very meaningful despite some hard-selling by its supporters.

An answer to this question is of particular importance when official policy is directed towards restricting wages to a certain level because of inflation. There may be a curb on dividends at the same time, but the end effect is to build up the industry's assets and investments so that, when the time for relaxation comes, it is the shareholder who benefits, both by an ultimate increase in dividend and by the increase in the value of his shares. This means that it is only the receiver of earned income who ultimately makes sacrifices—an unjust result by any standards.

The same is true in industries of innovation where, during the years of development, any profit must be ploughed back into the business for further R & D, and wages and dividends are held down. Ultimately, however, dividends are paid and, once again, the capital value of the shares has risen because of the increased assets of the company. Wage-earners, however, may get an eventual increase in money but they do not reap the benefit of the improvement in the company's status or get any compensation for the lean years. In both cases, income lost is lost forever.

There are two possible solutions to this injustice: first, deferred wages; where money wages are held to a specific level of increase by government policy, for example, but the company is in a position to pay more, the extra increase should not be lost to the workers but should accrue as equity in savings of the retained earnings, to become available at a later date when the economy is more stable or needs to be stimulated.

The second idea, and one which applies not only to wage restraint but to industries where profit is deferred for a number of years, involves the acquisition by workers of a share in the capital growth of a company. After wages have been negotiated, taking account of the needs of a worker in sustaining the living standards of himself and his family, there should be a further negotiation for a share of the cash flowing back into the company. This would have advantages for both management and workers, because the money would still be available to the company and would not restrict future growth and expansion, and the workers would have a right to a share in assets which they helped to create.

Workers have a moral and economic claim on the capital growth of a company; paid management already reaps the twofold advantage of income and capital assets in the combination of large salary and shares in the company through stock options. The risk-taking entrepreneur, who might be thought to have a moral right to the proceeds of growth in capital assets because of the risk involved, is no longer a feature of industrial life. Major firms are now public corporations, and it is arguable that the shareholder has, in fact, a lesser commitment to the industry than the workers in it, and certainly no moral right to a larger reward.

So far as decision-making at strategic level is concerned, the trade unions already have a considerable influence on industrial affairs through their representation on the National Economic Development Council and the twenty-one Economic Development Councils, or "little Neddies". These cover approximately two-thirds of the numbers employed in the private sector of industry. In them, as in the NEDC itself, representatives of the trade unions, government and management come together to discuss matters of general interest to industry. The members, because of the positions they hold in their respective industries, have considerable influence over the channels of communication, which is particularly important when it is exercised on attitudes and practices which may be recognized as holding back progress. But if the unions are to play their full part in the EDCs and in the Industrial Training Councils, which are organised on a similar basis, union leaders need to be as well equipped in sociological and management techniques as management themselves.

Conclusions

The years since 1964 have seen a new approach to industry by government, which is now committed to full partnership. The experience of the past few years suggests that industrial efficiency is the only effective route to economic growth. The machinery by which government can assist industry to become more efficient has been worked out, largely by trial and error, and with a rather disconcerting amount of error. The way is now clear for a more realistic partnership.

Much of what industry must do to become more efficient

must be done by industry from within, but the various advisory boards which government has provided can assist at all levels : NEDC, the EDCs, the CIR, the IRC, Industrial Training Boards, and the new Commission for Industry and Manpower. Government's main function is to see that these agencies know what their functions are and that they are properly equipped to perform them.

8

THE EUROPEAN SCENE

BRITAIN IS NOT the only European country where post-war governments, of whatever political colour, have felt that industrialists should not be allowed to operate in a totally "free" market. The need for direction, participation, direct intervention and distribution has impressed itself on successive finance and economic ministers in most continental countries.

Immediately after the war there was obviously a case for government resuscitation of private enterprise; many of the old manufacturers were dead or missing; many factories were gutted. A national policy was of paramount importance and countries like France were quick to see the need for concerted action from the centre, rather than piecemeal growth.

It might have been expected, however, that the scale of government intervention would lessen as each nation's economy made its recovery. In fact, the process of participation has gathered momentum, not lost it.

Italy, for instance, chose to bring up to date and expand the Institution for Industrial Reconstruction, first founded under the Mussolini government in 1933. France established her Commissariat au Plan. The Germans, perhaps because of their experience of excessive state intervention in the country's industry, were loth to tamper with private enterprise for many years, but have recently moved into the field. Sweden, despite being a model Social Democrat country, did little overt nationalizing, but has now accepted the need for restructuring, and established in January 1969 a Ministry of Industry run from within the Treasury.

The motive behind all this activity is obvious. At a time when US corporations are increasing their already massive holdings abroad, especially in the UK and on the mainland of Europe, national governments have a duty to see that their economy maintains a viable home sector, and does not become dominated by foreign firms, however paternalist in character.

The task of these governments is made all the more difficult by the often-fragmented nature of the basic industries to which the country looks for economic progress.

Nationalization of such assets has not been accepted as the answer to their industrial ills; persuasion, the setting of targets (as in France) and financial aid to company mergers or rationalization have been the usual methods.

But in recent years, and especially since the setting up of the British government-sponsored Industrial Reorganization Corporation, governments have become more discerning in their use of the tactics open to them. There is no doubt that the IRC has excited, if not admiration, considerable attention on the part of European governments.

Overseas representatives have consulted the IRC and examined its methods. Italian members of the Institution for Industrial Reconstruction travelled to the Corporation's Pall Mall headquarters and held a seminar with IRC executives, discussing the setting up of similar government-sponsored machinery in Italy. And in 1968, when the Swedes were in the preparatory stages of setting up a Ministry of Industry, they too asked for documentary evidence, and spoke to Corporation staff who were in Stockholm on IRC business. European observers have been anxious to examine what benefits in terms of increased efficiency have flowed from the Corporation's activities, and how they might revitalize their own industry to meet the challenge from other countries.

The French Fifth Plan to assess the growth of the chemicals industry concluded that, "An evolution of structures is also indispensable, for most foreign chemicals industries are much more concentrated than the French industry, and are made up of much larger companies. They can therefore afford more easily large scale investments and research, and to improve their

cost prices. To withstand this competition certain amalgamations are desirable between French firms during the next few
years."

A similar admission of the economic logic of government
intervention is provided by two schemes implemented by the
German government to reconstruct the country's mining and oil
companies. The German plans are the responsibility of the
Economic Minister, and are administered through existing
machinery. But method is not the key point: motive is, and
the motive in every case is the belief that governments can
and must have a role to play in making their industry more
efficient and competitive. Individual consideration of certain
countries will demonstrate the background to my thesis.

France

In 1947, the provisional government of the French Republic
decided to set up a modernization and equipment Plan. Crucial
problems facing the new Republic included lack of goods and
out-of-date equipment.

The thinking which lay behind the French proposal has been
described as a "development in thought paving the way for a
development in practice". The accent was on guidance, not
compulsion. Individual industries were told what their role was
to be in the nationwide effort to achieve a specific target.

The job of selling the national goal to management and
workers was given to M. Jean Monnet, at the head of the
Commissariat General au Plan, which later had Productivité
added to its title when that word became an international catch-
phrase. Using the slogan "concerted economy", Monnet urged
Frenchmen to unite in their efforts. Supporters of French-style
planning claim that he succeeded.

The Commissariat is small in numbers, comprising some forty
executives and other personnel totalling about one hundred.
Though it can co-ordinate planning it has no executive power.
Like the British NEDC, it has no cash resources. Again like
NEDC, it has twenty-seven modernization committees (or "little

Neddies") to advise it and its strength resides in the persuasive power of the economic arguments it puts forward.

The modernization committees are made up of from thirty to fifty unpaid people working together to produce a programme. The committee's personnel are drawn from the civil service, employers' organizations, senior ranks of management, and the trade unions. There is no fixed proportion of members from any one sector.

From the Commissariat, the plan goes to the Economic and Social Council (Conseil Supérieur du Plan) and Parliament. Though the first three plans were presented to these bodies as finished documents, the general direction of a new plan is now approved by the Conseil Supérieur, which therefore has to look twice at each plan : in its draft stage and when it is completed.

The French are proud that although there is no suggestion of compulsion in their planning, industrial units have in fact satisfactorily fulfilled the roles assigned them in the Fourth Plan. They have an interest in doing so. As one French economic commentator has pointed out : "The Plan holds out the prospect that, if everyone plays the game, each branch of production will find an effective market. It has two advantages, first of freeing the timorous from fear and secondly that of giving the rash food for thought."[1]

Rather than intervening directly in the affairs of individual firms, the State works by granting credits, tax exemptions and subsidies which are in line with the Plan.

The Fifth Plan, which runs from January 1966 to the end of 1970, envisaged an annual growth of 5 per cent a year, and a rise in consumption of $3\frac{1}{2}$ per cent. France was thus aiming at a cumulative growth of 27.5 per cent at the end of the five years.

One of the chief aims of the Plan is territorial development and planning, affecting West and South-West France, and the Massif Central. Land regrouping, the financial encouragement of farmers to give up their smallholdings to bigger units, and

[1]Firmin Oules, *Economic Planning and Democracy* (Penguin, trans. R. H. Barry), 1966, p.290.

industrialization are the strategies being used. In the South-West this means expansion of aeronautics; in Britanny the development of electronics, and in the North and East "industrial conversion" from the old-established industries of iron and coal, accompanied by manpower re-training.

On progress and productivity, the Plan points out that productivity is bound up with the size of the production unit. It adds: "One of the major tasks dictated by international competition is to encourage the formation and reinforcement of companies or groups of international dimensions, which alone can stand up successfully to foreign competition."

The Plan accordingly called for such groups—as few as one or two—in most major sectors of industry (aluminium, steel, motor manufacturing, chemicals, pharmaceuticals). Around these "great groups", which are intended to form the "backbone of the French industry of the future", are planned smaller firms specializing in high quality goods.

The future for small and medium-sized firms, says the Plan, is in conversion, specialization, or amalgamation with other businesses. The Plan, through the Ministry of Industry, offers "information and technical assistance" to facilitate these operations.

This offer, with no mention of hard cash to finance such structural changes, is an indication of the power of the Ministry of Industry. It has itself no authority to make grants; it can only recommend to the Ministry of Finance. It is this lack of financial authority which forms the basis of the case made by critics of French government in industry. What is the use, they say, of a Commissariat whose expansionist ideas are subject to the dead hand of the Treasury? But there are signs, detailed below, that the Finance Ministry is becoming more generous in its subsidies to industry.

A curious parallel is found between the French Plan's proposals for oil and the German plans. The Plan states: "France will continue to be supplied by the subsidiaries of the international oil groups, but the French firms as a whole are to form an organization of a size measuring up to the country's consumption. Their refining activities and distribution abroad will become equivalent to those of foreign industries in France. The tonnage of crude oil treated in France will rise from 53 million in 1964 to 85 million in 1970."

Preliminary results suggest that the Plan is working. Government-backed appointments at the top of the French banking system should promote a more copious flow of finance to industry for rationalization and mergers.

The Ministry of Industry has persuaded the Ministry of Finance to revitalize the main industries mentioned in the Fifth Plan. The chemical industry has been reduced to ten "great groups", and will be cut to five, no doubt "greater groups". Steel has been restructured to two basic groups, USINOR and SIDECO. Ministry of Industry plans to reduce the number of heavy mechanical engineering firms to ten or fifteen, await implementation.

The Treasury has provided a long-term loan of almost £200 million to the steel industry in exchange for rationalization of the out-of-date Lorraine works and the siting of new plant on the coast.

Regional development committees (CODERS) are at work and industrialists themselves are collaborating in regional expansion committees linked to the French Federation of Industry.

In Paris, the government's regional development department, DATAR (Delegation a l'Amenagement du Territorie et a L'Action Regionale), part of the Finance Ministry, is taking new industry to run-down areas, offering the usual tax, loan and investment incentives, and their efforts are backed by fifteen regional finance bodies (Societés de Dévoloppement Regional) formed about two years ago.

And finally there is the Fond de Développement Economique and Soniale (FEDS), which can grant additional long-term, low interest loans.

Whether all the aims of the Fifth Plan are achieved by late 1970 remains to be seen, but if past experience is anything to go by, they will. Having proved the efficacy of planning over two decades, it is surprising that the French were not first in the field with machinery on the lines of the IRC. They may yet follow suit.

Germany

Successive German post-war administrations have viewed government intervention in industry with great misgivings. The State has some nationalized interests. For instance, it owns 43 per cent of the shares of Lufthansa, the civil airline. The German government's hand, however, has been forced by the course of events.

First there was the problem of what to do with the mines. Collieries were in the hands of private ownership and were often operated in small, uneconomic units. They were incapable of producing sufficient coal at an economic price and they were very heavy on manpower. It is a tale very reminiscent of some British coalfields, with the difference that the owners were private companies.

The West German government has invested millions of Deutschmarks in a bid to resuscitate the industry, while still leaving it in private hands. The process began at the end of 1968 and is still going on.

The Federal Ministry of Economics is sponsoring the project, handled by a specially-created holding company. The government finances and supervises mergers on the basis of long-term loans. Funds are also available for retaining redundant miners, and the attraction of new industry to the districts aptly named "structural areas". The uneconomic pits are closed and a less cumbersome, more competitive industry is beginning to emerge.

The second German reconstructive effort also covers a valuable raw material: oil. Talks began in February 1969 to set up a national oil organization which would take in the country's eight major oil firms. The Bonn Government was prepared to put DM. 575 million (£57 million) into the organization over a six-year period to stave off the threat of the country's oil market being taken over by foreign companies. The market is currently dominated by the international American, Dutch and British firms, who account for 75 per cent of sales. Bonn's intention is to promote a private merger of the German oil companies to produce a single organization big enough to compete with the largest operators.

Germany, which has no oil of its own, could then establish its own oilfields and guarantee supplies in times of crisis. The national oil organization would trade under its own name and prospect as a subsidiary of the other eight companies. Funds would be made available for prospecting, buying up concessions, and participating in foreign oilfields.

The government was propelled into activity by a takeover bid by a French oil firm for the German oil company Gelsen-kichener Bergwerks A. G. (Gelsenberg). The French effort failed when the German utility concern R.W.E. (Rheinisch-West-faelisches Elektrizitaetswerk) took over a substantial holding in Gelsenberg.

The way was then clear for Economic Minister, Karl Schiller, to point out the vulnerability of the German oil industry to his cabinet colleagues.

Both the oil and mining restructuring programmes will take years, rather than months, to complete. They once again demonstrate the appeal of intervention in industry to govern-ments—even those normally anti-interventionist.

Italy

The basic machinery for promoting co-operation between government and industry in Italy is the IRI (Instituto per la Reconstruzione Industriale) established by decree on 23 January 1933, with an endowment fund of 895.4 billion lire.

The Institute's apologists claim that from the beginning it was no abstract concept or the result of deliberate directives. Rather, it was held to be the outcome of successive events and circumstances, economic and political.

It began as an emergency institution with a strictly financial role and was conceived as an instrument for rehabilitating and reforming the Italian banking system, which has developed since the turn of the century on the German "mixed" model.

In 1933, because of the Depression, the government decided to enter the hazardous field of industrial financing. IRI received vast numbers of shares and loans relating to the country's industrial system. The original idea was that the Institute should later gradually return to private control all industrial assets taken over from the banks.

Within three years, the government realized that private capital accumulation was insufficient to support further development of the economy *and* provide money to buy back from IRI the companies taken under the State umbrella. In later years, it became obvious that a return to the private sector of these firms was impossible, and it was after the war that the real growth in the Institute's holdings took place.

The IRI today is a very different body to that founded by the Fascist government. Some of the smaller private firms have been returned to private enterprise. Those still in public ownership have been expanded, and entirely new initiatives have been undertaken, in new fields—e.g. airlines, cement and motorways.

The IRI's present structure is divided into four main sectors:

1. Manufacturing: this comprises steel, engineering, shipyards, cement and a few small units in textiles and mining.

2. Public Utilities: this includes telephones, airlines, radio and television, and shipping.

3. Toll motorways: this covers both construction and management of toll-roads and is linked to the government's programme for creating a national motorways programme.

4. Credit sector: the banks reformed in 1933 and not returned to private ownership.

The Institute is continuing to diversify its operations as a state holding company, and it is playing a major role in the current 5-year plan, which ends in 1970. One of its chief aims is to reduce the industrial imbalance between North and South.

Figures for 1967 (the latest published in detail) show IRI holdings at 31 December of that year as:

	Total book value (million lire)
Banking and finance	187,945
Steel	171,025
Shipyards	69,154
Engineering	103,171
Telephones	148,883
Airlines	44,988
Shipping	17,630
Toll Motorways	10,546
Radio and Television	9,448
Miscellaneous	57,285
Total	820,075

There has been a phenomenal increase since 1933, as the figures show. But the IRI has many critics, who say it has become too institutionalized, too bureaucratic—and the tool of politicians. Too many local IRI offices, it is said, have become the headquarters of the area Socialist and Catholic parties; and too many new projects are undertaken because of the political kudos they bring to the proposer.

The IRI replies by saying that it is not linked to any given system of political thought, but works from pragmatic economic principles.

The Institute's sales in 1967 were 2,230 billion lire, an increase of 190 billion lire (9.3 per cent) on the previous year. Net profit was 154 billion lire.

Perhaps to answer its critics, IRI is now proposing the establishment of machinery on the lines of the IRC. It may be that economists inside the IRI want to get on with the job of restructuring industry unhindered by sectional political interests.

Whatever the motives, Italians will once again be taking the initiative in Southern Europe in institutionalizing a process which is commonly agreed exists and ought to be codified.

Sweden

Since 1 January 1969, the Swedish government has had a new Ministry of Industry, with one of the government's most successful young administrators in charge. It is part of the Ministry of Finance, which means that it generally avoids the drawback of financial impotence.

Its role may be described as something between the Department of Economic Affairs and the IRC. It is active in the restructuring of industry and also in raising finance for long-term propositions.

The lessons learned from the IRC are obviously being put into practice for evidently behind its setting up was the realization that economic competition from international firms was stiffening, and government-promoted changes in Swedish industry were necessary to ensure the competitive position of the country.

The economist Dr. Tore Browaldh, speaking to businessmen in May 1968, summed up the situation: "The American domination of certain sectors of the European market will probably result in a trend towards larger corporations. We shall probably see an increasing number of mergers. This is a development which will also involve Sweden. During the next five to seven years, many mergers will take place between corporations which by former standards were considered very large and financially sound".

He gave figures which showed that concentration had gone further in Sweden than anywhere else in Europe. The number of private-owned corporations with at least 500 employees was 293 in 1964, with a total of 735,000 employees—35 per cent of all workers.

Most of these firms were very small by international standards but the trend is there, and the government action is doubtless partly motivated by the desire to superintend more closely the privately-initiated mergers, as well as to exercise its own talents in that direction.

Other Countries

There are other industrialized countries in Europe which are faithful adherents of planning, especially the Netherlands. The common denominators in them all are fear of being swamped by more efficiently-organized foreign firms, and the need to restructure "tired" industries such as iron and steel and coal.

Holland and her neighbour Belgium have faced the latter problem in common with most coal-producing nations in Europe. The Dutch State mines have put through a programme of reconstitution, closing down unprofitable collieries and attracting alternative industry to the area. Similar work has been undertaken by the Economic Ministry in Belgium's steel-and-coal dominated East and South.

A Comparison of Industry and National Budgets

It may be useful, before leaving the different European patterns of government-industrial relations to illustrate the size and structure of the transnational firm in relation to national budgets. It is not simply that large firms spend more than some small countries, but it emphasizes again the importance of modern industrial power and therefore the need for a clear and recognizable dialogue between government and industry. The following table was prepared by the Ministry of Technology.

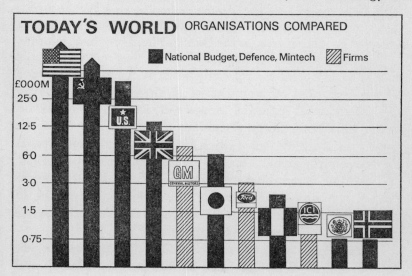

From left to right the columns on the chart represent :
The USA national budget (£72,000m.);
The national budget of the Soviet Union (£62,000m.);
The USA defence budget;
The UK national budget;
General Motors annual turnover;
The Japanese national budget;
Ford International annual turnover;
The French defence budget;
ICI annual turnover;
Mintech annual expenditure;
The Swiss National budget.

The supra-national company is likely to become an even more common feature of European life in the next decade. The necessity for European companies to compete for international markets and the threat of increased United States penetration of Europe suggest that the proposed merger of Dunlop and Pirelli is likely to be only the first of many such unions.

Straight mergers are likely to be limited by such factors as different tax structures and company laws, but combinations can be achieved by other means, as the Dunlop-Pirelli proposals indicate.

The concentration of industrial power raises numerous social and political questions, especially when it is not accompanied by any equivalent concentration of political power. The danger that international industrial groups will, in the not too distant future, grow more powerful than any one nation state is not the figment of a fevered imagination but a very real possibility, as the above table shows. There is a close link between economic and political power, and corporations whose annual turnover exceeds the national budgets of the individual countries in which they operate may well eventually consider themselves answerable to no one national government.

Governments, therefore, must consider the implications, not only of individual mergers such as that between Dunlop and

Pirelli, but also the longer term issues raised by the evolution of the multi-national corporation. If governments are to retain political control, they must find ways of acting together and must create political institutions capable of controlling the activities of the international giants.

The Future of Europe

But the evolution of the multi-national corporation is not the only problem which the governments of Europe must tackle together in the industrial field.

The above examination of individual European countries has made it clear that intervention in industry, in the form of nationalization or state financing, is common to most of Europe, while two countries, Sweden and Italy, are exploring the possibility of following Britain's example and extending the nature of government intervention through agencies similar to the Industrial Reorganization Corporation.

The question inevitably arises: is it enough for government involvement with industry to be restricted to activities within its national boundaries?

The answer must, I submit, be "No", and I make no apology for stating once again the reason why this is so: Europe must respond to the American challenge, and industry cannot meet this challenge without the intervention and assistance of the European governments working together.

All that has been said of the disparity between British and American achievement in the industrial field—the gap between the United States and the British achievement in applying technology to industry and the management gap especially—is equally true of Western Europe as a whole.

So far as the technological gap is concerned, the rest of Europe is in a worse plight than the United Kingdom, for Britain's Research and Development Budget of £1,000 million (2.3 per cent of the GNP) represents two-thirds of the total amount spent by Europe as a whole. Only France, the Netherlands and Western Germany (spending respectively 1.6, 1.9 and 1.4 per cent of their GNP) have made any conspicuous attempt to develop their technologies on a national basis. Germany's contribution has been handicapped by the limitations on their nuclear programme, while the Netherlands share is somewhat inflated, since it rests mainly on the R & D programmes of its industrial giants, Unilever, Philips and Royal Dutch.

The educational and management attitudes in Europe are, like those in Britain, the product of societies which have, for far too long, been closed, and partly static. The rise of a new young, vigorous management class has closed the gap considerably over the past ten years and a more dynamic approach is taking over, but much needs to be done before professional management is accepted without question as a matter of learned techniques and the only way to run industry efficiently.

Meanwhile, American influence spreads : world markets in many industries are dominated by United States corporations and their influence penetrates into Europe as companies such as Fords gain control of large sectors of key industries. American business is now a serious economic force in Europe, and there is a clear intention on the part of the American corporations to become the dominant force. This threat must be countered.

And it is not only the United States with whom European industry is in serious competition in world markets. Japan's rapid rise (based largely on the purchase of American technology) to near the top of the "league table" of world sales in motor cars, ships and electronics, is a further threat to the ultimate viability of European industry.

No one European nation can afford the kind of R & D budgets necessary to support industries which are to be viable in world markets : national technology is necessarily selective and important opportunities are lost. No one European country has a large enough home market to support industries of the necessary size to compete internationally : the American home market is one of the great strengths of American industry.

The answer to how European governments can promote European (including their own national) industries must lie in some kind of united response to the American challenge. What is this response to be?

One approach which has been the subject of much discussion is protectionism. This would involve repressive measures such as as legislation against American firms to prevent their gaining further footholds in Europe, and tariff restrictions.

The dangers of the protectionist approach can be clearly seen if one examines the Japanese computer industry. Japan is the only country other than Great Britain in which IBM, the US company, does not have more than 50 per cent of the computer market. This has been achieved not, as is the case with ICL, by concentrated R & D and the rationalization of the industry, but by government intervention to restrict the number of foreign computers sold in Japan. The effect on the Japanese computer industry is that there has been no incentive to rationalise: computers are still made by a number of firms, all of whom make all their own components and, although there is now a government sponsored research and development programme, the industry is characterised by fragmentation and duplication of effort. Should protection be withdrawn, and pressure for this is growing from the US, from whom most of the technology has been purchased, the Japanese industry will be in no fit state to compete.

Protectionist measures are, therefore, likely to be ineffective, and this is generally accepted. What is needed, if the effect of government intervention in this area is to be the strengthening of European industry, is a more positive response. Two areas which would be particularly susceptible to co-operation between European governments are management education and technological research.

Management Education

European universities have been slow to provide masters' degrees in business administration or to set up research departments. This has led to a general shortage of teaching staff in this subject, so that, although business schools now exist all over Europe, they are not enough to cope with the demand which exists for management education. In France, for example, the system can only cope with a tenth of the demand.

Research facilities, especially, are limited by this shortage of teachers, so that the actual quality of the management education available improves hardly at all. Further difficulties are encountered by such international schools as INSEAD, the European Institute of Business Studies, who are unable to persuade enough companies to open their files to provide case studies for academic work. The result is that much of the teaching in the European schools is based on American practice, which is not always precisely applicable to European companies, especially in so far as economic dissimilarities such as the slow development of the European industrial state and the greater dependence of Europe on exports and tax and legal systems are concerned. Graduates of the European business schools tend, therefore, to be better equipped to manage American companies than European ones.

Professional management is especially necessary in those industries where scientific advance has led to the introduction of new techniques; rapid application and adaptation of such techniques is of vital importance to economic development.

The proposal for an International Institute for the Management of Technology now being considered by an OECD Working Party under the Chairmanship of Sir John Chadwick is, therefore, an especially valuable and welcome one.

The Institute, after a considerable debate, is to be set up in Milan with a nucleus of internationally known teachers. It will be financed by the adherent countries in proportion to their national revenues and by subscription fees from private participants, whose inclusion is considered to be of equal importance with that of governments. There will be a General Council, on which members will vote according to their shareholding, which will decide general strategy for the Institute and appoint the Board of Directors and the General Manager who will be concerned with the day-to-day running of the Institute.

It will aim, through teaching and research programmes, to stimulate the study of complex technological problems. It will also study methods designed to promote the entire process of innovation and teaching forecasting techniques which can be used as a basis for decisions in the development and management of new technologies. Another aim will be to make top management sensitive to and well informed on the development and conduct of technological innovation. It is hoped that it will rapidly become the focus of international discussions on the subject and a meeting point for representatives of both industry and government at international level.

The programme consists of two types of intensive courses: the first on general problems of management and on more particular problems (for example, the use of electronic computers in firms or problems concerning multi-national enterprises), are designed for top management; advanced courses on specific problems such as decision techniques, forecasting, planning, operation research and the like, are meant to give complete mastery of these techniques in discussion and will include studies of actual cases. Regular courses, lasting a full academic year, will give a complete picture of modern management techniques in the field of technological innovation.

There will also be a research programme to cover all aspects of the Institute's activities, forming the necessary integration of the teaching activity, especially so far as the study of specific problems is concerned. The contents of the courses will change from year to year as the Institute accrues experience and changes in requirements.

The International Institute for the Management of Technology is an excellent example of what can be done in this field by governments working together to make the best use of their resources. The proposal that the private sector should be able to participate on a subscription basis underlines the need for governments and industry to work in partnership in this area.

Research and Development

There is even more need for collaboration between governments in the field of scientific research and technological development. There is no lack of scientific talent in Europe and this is an area in which Britain has much to offer. (It was an American, John Rhodes, who pointed out that the basic inventions which have made possible American advances such as the "Jumbo" jet and the Apollo space programme, the jet fighter aircraft and the large liquid-fuelled rocket, were European.)[1]

But Europe must rationalize its resources. Much of the R & D undertaken in Western Europe is duplicated, adding to the problems of the "technological gap", which is further increased by the apparent inability of the European nations to exploit invention.

This "gap" must be an important issue in any discussion of European industry and technology. It might be supposed that the European Economic Community would provide a means of reducing it since it provided not only a tariff free area but also an economic union, which logically ought to lead to greater specialization and less wasteful duplication.

Until recently, however, this was not the case. The nation states of Europe have devoted the greater part of their effort in new technology to purely national programmes so that even in fields where other treaties, such as the one which brought Euratom into existence, operated, no joint programme was achieved. Euratom achieved less in the nuclear energy field than the United Kingdom achieved on its own.

The past year, however, has seen the members of the European Economic Community wake up to the problems which confining scientific research within national borders brings. The Member States have recently concluded that the large-scale development of scientific and technological research, the constantly increasing size of the resource involved, and the advances outside Europe, make it necessary to adopt some form of co-operation. A Working Party of experts was instructed to study the possibilities, beginning with the fields of information science, telecommunications, the development of new means of transport, oceanography, metallurgy, environmental pollution and meteorology. A study of the Working Party's report, the Aigrain Report, by the Member States, produced a large measure of agreement as to the importance and urgency of many

[1] John Rhodes, *The American Challenge Challenged,* Harvard Business Review, 10 September 1969.

of the proposed activities, and Britain, although not a member of the EEC, was asked to participate in the co-operation, an invitation which was promptly accepted. This is a constructive and promising development.

Projects under consideration range from studies, lasting only a few months—both exploratory and designed to investigate prospects for more major activities—to public and research projects of a basic or preliminary nature, dealing with such things as standardization, and to industrial projects aimed at developing new products or materials.

Projects will be implemented through industry, both public and private, through the use of existing centres, national as well as international, and through concerted action, a form of international co-operation, whereby the individual programmes and budgets of participants will be co-ordinated at international level by a committee of participants.

At the beginning of 1970 the Aigrain Committee began work in earnest. The seven sectors of co-operation already agreed on gave rise to forty-seven proposals for joint action, and a comparison of a national research and scientific budget is in preparation. This part of its work, which is without any doubt the most important, should result in the definition of new fields of co-operation.

The Aigrain Committee provides a solid, practical example of what European politicians can achieve when they abandon idealistic talk of the European dream and get down to practicalities.

A similar, less formal, approach has been adopted by the European parliament. Three years ago the Parliament, through its Science Committee under the Chairmanship of Victor Leemans, a Belgian Senator and former President of the European Parliament, broke through its formal links with governments and initiated discussions with a group of parliamentarians.

The aim was to explore ways of scientific and technological collaboration, and since that time meetings have taken place at regular intervals in both Brussels and London, even during the times when Britain's relationship with the rest of Western Europe has been strained. Specialist advice has been taken from leading industrialists and scientists and a number of specific "industries of innovation" are now under examination, notably cryogenics, inter-city transport systems, oceanography and VTOL/STOL aircraft. Without wishing to overstate the value of such informal approaches, it would be said that they have paved the way for future formal approaches to the technological problems facing Europe.

A further idea which has been canvassed, notably by the British Prime Minister, Harold Wilson, in 1966, is that of setting up a European Technology Community. Unfortunately, the structure and purpose of such a community was never properly defined, but, to succeed, it would have to have a European R & D Budget and decisions would have to be taken by a directorate on behalf of all the member states. It would promote centres like CERN at Geneva, and would no doubt make a valuable contribution on the scientific side but, without economic or market backing, it would not make any inroads in meeting the American threat at the point where the need for co-ordination is most urgent, the application of science. At present, the Aigrain Committee approach seems most likely to succeed.

The Implications of European Co-operation

If Western Europe succeeds in co-ordinating its technological effort, the demand for it to be translated into commercial terms should quickly follow. In fact, the demand could be said to have preceded it, for its results will be more mergers of the Dunlop-Pirelli trans-frontier kind.

One candidate for rationalization on a European basis is the computer industry. The record of ICL is excellent, as the case study showed, but if the company is to maintain its performance it needs other manufacturing units and outlets in Europe, while the European computer industry would benefit from ICL's research and development programme. Similar considerations apply to other industries. World competition is forcing down prices in some mechanical and engineering sectors. Larger units would eliminate duplication in such areas as distribution and marketing enabling increased sales and production to offset the trend. But there is a limit to expansion where it is restricted by national frontiers. It is in this area that the managing director of the IRC thinks that a European IRC could function, to re-organize and restructure Europe's most vulnerable industries.

As I pointed out above, mergers producing multi-national companies have their dangers as well as their benefits. For this reason there is a movement within the EEC to give the EEC Commission the power to police industrial mergers and take-overs, particularly those involving bids from foreign-based or overseas companies.

The evolution of the supra-national company must also, eventually, lead to the development of some degree of inter-national agreement on such things as company law. Rapid agreement or even progress in this area is unlikely—the problem of matching different legal systems is extremely complex but it is, nevertheless, one which must be solved if real progress is to be made. The pressures on the government-industry relation-ship are the same internationally as they are nationally, and solutions to these problems will have to be found. The draft convention creating a European Patent discussed last year by representatives of seventeen European countries, is therefore to be welcomed as a step in the right direction.

Conclusion

The breaking down of the present barriers between nations, with ultimate harmonization of taxation and company laws, is a distant and daunting prospect. But the prospect of, say, an inter-nationally-organized steel industry offers scope for production and efficiency on a scale that makes restructuring within national boundaries look pale. The way would be open for continental-sized European firms able to compete on more equal terms with such American giants as General Motors, IBM, and Boeing.

And, just as in Britain and other European nations, govern-ments have been compelled by events to initiate change, so it will be in the case of trans-national co-operation.

9

RE-DEFINING THE PARTNERSHIP

THE PATTERN OF government-industrial relations has
repeatedly been shown to be one of peaks and troughs rather
than of continual improvement. Changes have not been confined
to any particular government or period. Wartime conditions and
the necessity for speedy, urgent measures and common standards
have contributed as much as Labour governments, whose influence has not been as extensive as either critics or supporters
make out.

The attitudes of the political parties to government involvement in industry have been characterized by inconsistency. The
reaction of the Tories to the proposed Industrial Relations Bill
with its penal clauses showed that they wanted more intervention, not less.[1] Labour—interventionist on grants, subsidies,
and regional aid—did not want this kind of intervention, though
after bitter debate. Political parties, it seems, are not a reliable
indicator of public opinion on this matter; if, in fact, there is
a consensus at all.

Industry, representing a vast network of businesses, has fallen
back on the CBI as its mouthpiece, and it has issued statements
whose tone seems designed to antagonize any government, however well-disposed. The communications system existing between
government and industry is far from being ideal, or even adequate, and improvements are unlikely while there is an absence
of mutual trust.

Some commentators would agree with Mr. Enoch Powell that
a total clash between government and industry is inevitable

[1] A Conservative Political Centre Pamphlet *Change or Decay* (No. 268,
1963), argued that modern industry cannot operate independently of
Parliament and suggested ways of closer integration between the two.

and even in some respects, desirable. Others propose that the two should work in isolation. Even assuming this were possible, it is doubtful whether modern industry could begin to "go it alone". The many reasons which operate against this have already been examined, but it is worth re-stating here why industry needs the support of government :

(*a*) the scale of business, especially that involving the more advanced sectors of technology, is now so vast and complex that individual firms outside the United States are not able to meet the cost themselves, and therefore need government support at the research and development stage;

(*b*) although there has been a scaling-down of tariff barriers in Europe with the various economic alignments, trade in capital goods is affected by administrative preferences which operate in favour of the national suppliers. This means that the drive on the export markets for the advanced technological products demands the combined resources of industry and Whitehall;

(*c*) the full range of supporting government grants is intended to stimulate not only the firm receiving the aid, but the economic health of a region or an industry.

What can be done to improve the quality of government-industry relations? I have argued that, provided we can be certain that management in industry will tackle its own restrictive practices and will work hard to develop effective operational standards, government intervention should be reduced.

On the government side the answer lies on several fragmented fronts, but all underlining the need for change and improvement.

Changes Within the Government System

Improvements in government decision-making are not dependent on party politics. There have been cases within the past twenty-five years of competent, progressive Ministers who could hold their own with the best senior executives in the top American firms, but there have also been men in charge of industrial and economic departments who were at best inadequate and were known to be so. Such appointments can only be explained in terms of the balancing act which a Prime Minister normally tries to perform in dispensing his patronage, and such contortions are certainly not confined to one party alone.

Furthermore, Ministers hold office for a relatively short time, which is in many respects a good thing, but it does mean that few changes in the way in which government takes decisions can be expected to result from the work of individual Ministers.

Improvements in the decision-making process must come, therefore, from the administration. It may take ten to fifteen years for there to be any improvement in the quality of politicians, but this will not matter half so much as long as the necessary changes in the Civil Service can be fully implemented within the next three years. The integrity and devotion of the civil servants is not in question, but, as I have pointed out, their training and personnel development has failed to keep pace with the industrial and sociological changes. The experience of Japan and America is relevant here: in these countries the civil servant is encouraged to build up his own work team, often with men and women from the best of the industrial organizations, whilst he himself will be expected to move into a key post in industry when he is about forty or fifty. It is this interchange between industry and government which is recognized as being so important, and it seems to me to be a practice which Britain could profitably adopt.

The recommendations of the Fulton Report, if fully implemented, could turn the Civil Service into the efficient tool of government which it ought to be.

I have already suggested that a moratorium should be declared on changes in government structure, especially as the basis now seems to meet the model requirements of the Haldane Committee. I would also suggest that questions concerning the allocation of functions should in future be referred to an all-Party Committee on the structure of government. It is an axiom of industry that rarely can today's managers in a large undertaking effectively influence today's profits; it is equally true that government decisions will more significantly affect the economy of the future than of the present. Changes in function and new factors can only be dealt with on a long-term basis if there is some over-all plan and the promise of stability for the future.

The illogical way in which a subject can be distributed between a number of departments under the present system can be seen in relation to a prices policy. The lack of a co-ordinated approach by government has made a mockery of its good intentions in the prices and incomes field. The situation as it exists today is totally unsatisfactory. The Department of Employment and Productivity has general responsibility for carrying out the prices and incomes policy, and therefore responsibility for referring price cases to the PIB. However, it has no direct function that relates to prices and no source of direct information about them. The functions and the information belong to no less than fourteen production departments, three (until recently four) of which (Board of Trade, Ministry of Technology and Power, and the Ministry of Fisheries and Food), have an interest in prices. None of them, however, has a direct interest in a prices policy or in general price stability, and none of them is big enough in impact on the economy for the level of prices and services within its responsibility to determine the whole. Information about prices too is dispersed in all three departments. By contrast, information and policy on incomes is the concern almost entirely of the Department of Employment and Productivity. Income cases pass more readily and rationally through the machinery; perhaps prices cases might as well, if there were one department responsible, equipped with the necessary expertise and information. The DEP's new responsibility for the work of the Monopolies Commission and the Restrictive Practices Court may help here, but it is only a very small step in the right direction. It would be possible to cite hundreds of similar examples of this kind, covering every department of government.

Some commentators will argue that industrial affairs can be quite well looked after by inter-departmental committees; these, however, do not have the drive and sense of urgency which is always possible in a single department-based committee. Much time is lost in delineating the exact responsibilities of each department involved. The time and energy wasted by inter-departmental committees seems to have been one of the strongest motivating factors behind the 1969 reorganization of the departments of government concerned with industry.

Whether this reallocation of functions between the Board of Trade and the Ministry of Technology with its new responsibility for power is adequate to meet the demands of the situation remains to be seen. I would have preferred to see the "science" sector of the Department of Education allocated to the Ministry of Technology as well. The emphasis in the new Board of Trade should be more commercial than hitherto, now that so many of the activities accumulated over the years, more as a reflection on the power and prestige of past incumbents of the office of President than with any regard to logic, have passed to depart-ments better qualified to deal with them.

Then there is the relationship of the two Ministries, Mintech and the Board of Trade, with Treasury and general economic planning. The abolition of the Department of Economic Affairs was one which I welcomed, but the reallocation of its function was not all that could be desired. Responsibility for the National Economic Development Council has passed to the Cabinet Office; medium and long-term planning have passed to the Treasury, who have responsibility for co-ordinating consultation between Departments and industry on some aspects of the work of NEDC; other industrial functions, e.g. regional economic development, have gone to Mintech. It could be argued that there should be only two departments in the industrial-economic field—a combination of Mintech and the Board of Trade and the Treasury, but I believe this would result in too large a concentration of responsibility for efficiency. A combination of Mintech and the Board of Trade would mean a staff of over 50,000.

If government machinery is made more efficient it will go a long way to resolving the present conflicts and ineptitude in decision-making. I have already mentioned the importance of the techniques of performance such as management-by-objectives, but a positive incentive is also required by which every employee from Under-Secretary downwards would be encouraged to economise on manpower and waste. This raises questions of financial control. It is clear that the present system, whereby a department which underspends in one financial year has an equivalent sum deducted from its grant for the following year, is likely to encourage a department head to refrain from listing his spare resources!

Two ways of making the system more *operationally* effective would be the use of tried techniques of measurement and control and the greater use of the knowledge of the social scientists in both administrative and executive areas.

Measurement and control techniques (apart from those applied to individual performance mentioned above) would cause systematic re-classification of the functions involved and services provided. A major task in the next decade will be a method study of the total system of government. In effect an appraisal of the system will ensure that the aims and purposes of the function of administration are being questioned. It has been found too often in industry that the desire for more effective methods of work has concealed the need for a major review of the aims and objectives of an organization. In the Civil Estimates presented to parliament by government departments, for instance, there are general and unrevealing categories of expense like "General Administration" running to many millions of pounds. MPs and the electorate want to know what this money is actually for. David Howell, a determined and thoughtful MP, has argued that if matters like this could be clarified there would be a number of policy choices open to the politician. "The choice would be for him to look at a mass of Government services and functions and to decide on the basis of accurate cost and benefit assessment",[1] which should be given support. I accept this and will argue below the need for more parliamentary involvement, but the case for operational techniques stands on its own and is directly related to the need for the organization to be more effective. In Germany, government accounts are now

[1] D. Howell, *Controlling Public Spending: a time for new techniques*, Moorgate & Wall Street Review, Spring 1969.

to be presented on the basis of functions rather than institutions. In other words, instead of half-a-dozen departmental figures having to be extracted and collated in order to grasp the total cost picture of a particular government policy, there will be a statement of accounts within a particular function.

As I have already pointed out, intelligent use could be made by governments of the whole field of knowledge covered by the term "social science". It is used broadly to include all the major disciplines that deal with group and individual behaviour —anthropology, economics, history, political science, psychology, and sociology—and those aspects of other disciplines, such as geography, psychiatry, and linguistics, that have behavioural dimensions. So little is known of social science in Britain that I would propose a detailed inquiry, similar to one undertaken in the United States, to examine how the knowledge and methods of the social scientist can be effectively applied to the programmes and policy processes of government.

In the United States, a special committee was set up by the National Academy of Sciences—National Research Council (NAS–NRC) in 1965, to assess how far government policies and programmes could be improved by the introduction of the social sciences. Stimulus was given to the NAS–NRC by the controversial Project Camelot, an Army-supported study of social change in Latin America. In the years that followed, the committee has investigated foreign area research (published by NAS–NRC) in 1967 and brought together in a major conference government officials, academic social scientists and representatives from private and research organizations. In addition to the committee's investigation, several Congressional inquiries into government programmes in the social sciences have looked at their effectiveness and quality.

The specific areas of an inquiry in this country might include some of the following:

1. To what extent are social scientists as a group used by government departments? As individuals making a contribution to teams of research workers? What support is there among top administrators in the Civil Service for the idea of using social

sciences and to what extent do they appreciate their relevance to the policies and programmes for which they are responsible?

2. What proposals can be made to attract social scientists into the government service and what incentives and opportunities can be introduced for the implementation of their findings?

3. To what extent are joint projects undertaken with other countries, such as the US, on urban development, communications and social development? A great deal of duplicated effort could be saved if joint research were undertaken by various co-operating countries.

The answers to such questions will enable an assessment to be made of the usefulness of the social sciences in government but would also be some way towards appraising the processes of research and decision-making in government. The gap between the two is wider than it should be. Furthermore, the range of social science inter-disciplinary teams is enormous; they can provide not only basic knowledge and new material but also insights of great value relative to policy decisions and practical affairs from child-rearing to national defence.

Changes Within the Industrial System

Industry can do a good deal on its own to further its relations with government, primarily by improving internal communications. In the first place, there is no doubt that as units become larger, structural and informational problems will become more complex, so that mergers and expansion generally will have to be carefully planned and managed. Mergers may be justified on financial or organizational grounds, but they raise serious problems of communication both for the manager of the taken-over firm and its new owners. The debate in the textile industry, involving the big four companies, highlights the very attractive possibilities of rationalizing an industry which needs a stronger base both here and in Europe.

I recently directed a research project[1] at the University of

[1] E. Moonman, *Communication in an Expanding Organization*, Tavistock, 1970.

Manchester which looked at some of the human relations problems associated with mergers in this very industry. There are
some areas of this inquiry which may startle rather than reassure
anyone who has not been in the position of being taken over.

Management has to be willing and able to take action of
the right kind, and relationships within the firm must be such
that the action taken is acceptable and is fully understood. This
implies a constant exchange of ideas and attitudes between all
levels of staff, a particularly difficult state of affairs to maintain
after a merger.

If bitterness and mistrust have built up, it almost always pays
for the new holding company to undertake an attitude survey,
preferably using outside consultants or researchers who are more
likely to produce frank responses than the average manager.
The research team at Manchester unearthed deep anxiety among
staff in the companies investigated, some of which were very
recent acquisitions of the group, about the failure of communications at all levels.

One example is this extract from an interview with a top
executive with twenty years' service :

"Communication is bad—couldn't be worse. Indeed it has
never been worse. In a long association with the company I am
surprised to find that communication at all levels is so vague and
uncertain. The top executives just seem unable to deal with the
needs and interests of all people below them."

Shop floor attitudes were expressed even more forcibly. A
selected group of employees was asked to define phrases
commonly used in industry and by the government, such as
"productivity must improve" and "personnel management". Of
the replies 75 per cent bore almost no relation to the phrases'
actual meaning. Productivity meant "outside management",
"work", "the boss", "the government", "an American method
of work", and personnel management meant a body "appointed
by the government", "to help management's problems", or "jobs
for the boys".

This textile group had grown to such a size that obviously
the vital activity of communication as disclosed by the research

would have to cease to depend on the unplanned activity of individuals, however well-meaning and enlightened. The process of passing on information must be as efficient as any production process.

I took the inquiries a step further by suggesting a tool which management might use to help employees play a constructive part when changes are proposed. It was felt that a meeting of representatives from all parts of the group would help them to feel a sense of "belonging" to the group, and would enable problems which might have cropped up elsewhere in the group, as well as policies, to be discussed. It was recommended that a system of meetings, to cut across existing levels of authority, should be set up and maintained.

They were to be purely advisory, for discussing, imparting, and feeding-back information. The pilot meeting which was held while the research was going on, confirmed the need for discussions between employees from different parts of the group and emphasized their importance as a communication technique. It was also felt that such meetings could be a useful training device for those who took part; training in the presentation of facts, both to the meetings and to the division as feed-back, and in group behaviour.

Communication is a continual process and requires close attention by all levels of management and in all types of organizations. In a business subject to intense pressure of change, such as at a time of merger, all the weaknesses will be exposed and slipshod management penalised.

The problem of communication is equally serious for the trade union movement. Reference has already been made to the need for new information systems within companies to involve the employee, and this will clearly provide the shop floor steward with new responsibilities and duties. If he is to do his job properly, administrative reforms are required within the union itself. This means better educational and research facilities; otherwise it will be increasingly difficult to obtain effective co-operation from the shop floor in national economic planning and in the introduction of new kinds of mechanisation. Changes

7—RP * *

are also required of a more fundamental nature, such as the merging of unions so as to reduce the conflict caused by demarcation disputes, and the cumbersome collective bargaining structure.

I believe that industry should, in general, continue to be allowed to bring about its own improvements. Employers, however, have an ambivalent attitude towards government involvement. It is best summed up as: "We want government money but not its influence." The best example of this arises in connection with trade and technological collaboration. Agreements were signed by the UK government with a number of Eastern European countries, the idea being that the governments would take the necessary formal steps and better relations and trade would follow. Some British firms have followed the government's lead; ICI and Courtaulds in particular have trade arrangements with Eastern Europe. But I have met a large number of executives who demand that our government should do more in the way of guarantees *before* they act. Surely this is a case where governments can encourage but where marketing success is the responsibility of the firm. The matter is so serious that I am convinced that trade could be doubled if British businessmen were to show more imagination in interpreting the technical agreements with the five countries concerned.[1] When I visited these five countries recently, the need for a more dynamic British approach was stressed everywhere. An official responsible for the Brno Trade Fair said, with disgust: "A large British company withdrew its sole representative from our country because they had not had anything to show for having spent £500. Three months later, the Czech government passed on a contract worth several million pounds to a rival firm in West Germany."

The importance of patience as well as determination was also stressed many times throughout our talks, and in view of the considerable difficulties in financial arrangements and travel regulations, as well as the language barrier, these are necessary virtues.

[1]Bulgaria, Czechoslovakia, Hungary, Poland and Rumania.

Although not directly mentioned in the technical agreements, improved trading relationships were expected. I was left in no doubt that, in all five countries, the agreements have contributed to the extension of some markets and the opening of others. The main trading in East Europe is, of course, between the countries themselves, but outside this bloc the UK is an important customer.

There are, unfortunately, many examples of British companies too idle to care, but there are also one or two shining examples of a well-thought-out approach. In Czechoslovakia, for instance, Courtaulds reached an agreement covering machinery as well as a package training and development programme for Czech technicians.

International Computers, in spite of French competition, has really proved its ability to get into and stay in the market, by acting on intelligent forecasting and by offering flexible terms. ICL has many key members of staff available at the end of a local phone call, and the outlook for our third generation machines seems favourable in Czechoslovakia, Poland and Hungary.

In short, industry has a right to expect far-sighted government planning and some consistent policies. But it should make a more enthusiastic effort to understand the workings of government by allowing a greater movement of staff between government and industry, as recommended by Fulton. It should receive adequate notice in which to consider the government's industrial strategy on matters ranging from taxation to trade agreements. But British industry should by now begin to see that it has to co-operate fully with whatever government is in power, for their mutual good. Too many firms examine government policies to see how they can prosper in spite of them instead of helping to initiate them. It is useless for them to mark time, hoping for a return to Conservatism and comparative laissez-faire. My view is that the Tory Minister of Industry will not alter much of the existing legislation affecting industry, apart from the area of collective bargaining, and it is quite conceivable that a slight turn of the economic screw administered by the Tories would see the small or medium sized firm in serious trouble.

The ideal role for the modern government is that of strategic planner, but it is frankly dangerous for it to start meddling in the tactics of management. There is no evidence of the necessity for more government control in industry. It is important, however, that a serious impartial assessment of all the existing degrees of intervention and sponsorship should be undertaken to see whether we can get the balance right. A philosophy on the subject is too much to expect but a consistent policy would be a reasonable aim.

The Role of Parliament

As we have seen, there are more than two participants in government-industrial relations. The parliamentary institution itself can play a vital role in judging the performance of both sides. The individual MP is, of course, relatively powerless to bring about change in this respect, but given increased status and proper research and advisory support, could be very influential.

A unique example of the parliamentarian's role in this is provided by the controversy aroused by Ian Mikardo's Select Committee on Nationalized Industries. For many years the Commons Select Committees on the Estimates and on Public Accounts have exercised a check over the direct expenditure of government departments. The Select Committee on Nationalized Industries investigated the public corporations, such as the National Coal Board, the airways corporations, British Rail, and so on. But there are quite large areas of public enterprise where Ministers exercise control and spend a lot of money but which are neither government departments nor public corporations, and in these areas the Ministers are free of any surveillance by MPs.

At the beginning of the 1967/68 parliamentary session, the Committee attempted to extend the list of bodies it could investigate, and a battle with the Treasury followed. Eventually the Committee were offered a group of thirty-four public bodies to examine but they were adamant that they wanted to include the Bank of England, Cable and Wireless, and British Petroleum. An unsatisfactory compromise was worked out but this case does reveal the difficulties of exposing the system of government to inquiry. Of course, it may be argued that if all those who had an interest in government were to be given rights of inquiry, it would make the actual mechanics of working almost impossible. A balance is needed. At the same time, substantial material can be produced by the parliamentary select committees, despite their slender resources. The Select Committee on Science and Technology, whose reports on the nuclear power industry were considered in Chapter V, is a good example. The Mikardo Committee is another; its first report (1967/68) put forward a closely argued case for a Ministry of Nationalized Industries which prompted the government to reply with a White Paper. They rejected this recommendation to unify all the nationalized industries under a single Ministry, but they accepted another of the Committee's recommendations :

"The government believe that within the existing pattern of responsibilities the tasks of particular departments require further detailed study. They therefore accept the Committee's recommendation that discussions should be held between the Treasury, the DEA and the Departments to clarify their respective contributions to the control of investment. Because of the importance of investment as a central feature of Ministerial control over the industries, the government believe this to be a most important recommendation."[1]

In order to overcome some of the problems in the future, and to give the committees more teeth, I advocate that they should be directly related to a research and information body.

In the central area of economic management, I would propose that the incipient CIM be linked to a House of Commons Specialist Committee which could follow up its findings. There is little of this kind of activity at present. In the four years of the PIB's existence (up to August 1969) more than 120 reports were

[1] *Ministerial Control of the Nationalized Industries*, HMSO, Cmnd. 4027, May 1969.

published; its main contribution has been to ask awkward questions; it has challenged complacent assumptions; for instance the report on the engineering industry revealed the way management had lost control over the wage structure, with the result that there was little relationship between performance and pay.

The CIM will have, as the PIB has, professional staff to carry out effective analysis and consultancy. Linking it with a Commons Committee could add to its authority and provide a follow-through. It would incidentally also give a stimulus to the Commons Committee system. No doubt other agencies could be similarly linked with committees.

It is only by means of such involvement that industrial personnel of high quality will eventually be persuaded to allow their names to go forward for parliamentary candidatures. The MP's job does not attract top executives for a variety of reasons, including the vulnerability of tenure, the absurd office facilities, and the complete lack of serious secretarial support. In my view, the most fundamental reason is the feeling, which I regret to say is quite valid, that the actual duties do not justify the effort of their execution. It has been pointed out to me by a number of managers, representing both the Tory and the Labour outlooks, that they were more likely to have an influence on major national decisions by working within their own industrial firms or institutes than by wasting their time on the back benches or even in a junior government post. Some argue that there are already people of talent representing industry in the House. This is to some extent true. In 1959, the occupational background of more than one in five MPs could be classified under the heading "business"—but this is not to say that they have had experience of large-scale operational or manufacturing industry.[1] My estimate is that in the 1966-70 parliament no more than a dozen MPs out of 630 had had any top-line management experience or had had to work through major management problems against a background of typical organizational conflict.

The trade unions, too, should encourage their ablest young

[1]Butler and Rose, *The British General Election of 1959*, Macmillan, 1960.

people to go into parliament, in preference to the present policy of rewarding a retiring or middle-aged officer for services rendered with a safe seat. It is against this background of the MP's job and its usefulness to himself, as an individual, that I would further justify the specialist committee system, as well as improvements in the services and facilities of the House of Commons.

Informing the Public

Increasing public interest in government policies has led to a demand for more public consultation and explanation of the administrative processes. The trend in recent years has been to satisfy this demand by wider and more open consultation before decisions are taken, and by providing the public with fuller information as to the basis on which decisions are made. The Labour government attempted to meet this need in two main ways:—the release of more factual information and the publication of data referred to in forecasting.

More factual information is being disclosed in the form of descriptive material and statistics, particularly in the areas of science and technology. For example, the development of the Central Statistical Office and of the Government Statistical Service has been important because more statistics are provided and the methods and concepts behind them are explained so as to make them more useful to the government, industry and the community. Among the forthcoming statistical publications by the Statistical Office are a *Handbook of Statistics* which will present the most important series in an easily usable form, and *Social Trends* (a parallel publication to *Economic Trends*), designed to give a regular comprehensive statistical picture of social conditions. There is also increasingly close consultation between government statisticians and users of their publications; hence, the Statistics Working Party of the Confederation of British Industry is a valuable forum for such discussions in the early stages of the development of new plans.

There has also been a greater readiness to publish forecasts and other considerations involved in policy decisions—forward-looking assessments of public expenditure, more information on the economics and policies of the nationalized industries, full reports on Civil Service reforms. A case in point is the publication of background information concerning the Budget. In the Financial Statement accompanying the Budget in March 1968 the Chancellor published, for the first time, an economic forecast for the following fifteen months bearing on measures contained in the Budget. In 1969 he took the process further and in addition to the forecast for up to mid-1970 he included a reconciliation between the year's forecast and the actual return. An example in the wider economic field was the publication by the Department of Economic Affairs of *The Task Ahead*. The assessment in this paper was fully discussed in the National Economic Development Council enabling the government to take advantage of opportunities for informed consultation provided by that body. There are other more formal ways in which public discussion on an informed basis is encouraged before a decision is taken. In the siting of a new town, for instance, it is usual to publish a report by the planning consultants setting out the reasons for choosing a particular site, and then to invite representation at a public inquiry.

There is now such a wealth of statistical material that guidance is necessary on its details. *Statistical News,* which has been published quarterly by the Central Statistical Office since 1968, was founded for this purpose. It includes articles on major activities such as the new system of industrial statistics, invisible earnings and payments, input-output analysis, and so on. It also contains short notes of current developments and therefore provides a guide to changes in official statistics. The Central Statistical Office and other statistical departments are planning other publications with the same purposes; these will include, guides, lists of publications and series, and explanatory leaflets on the use and limitations of particular series.

Despite these advances in public consultation, and they are definite advances, the government is still inclined to over-emphasize the need for caution. For instance, there have been justified complaints that the government withheld information on why it decided against participation in the (CERN) 300 GeV machine. Many scientists take the view that the Department of Education and Science concealed from the rest of the government the weight of professional opinion. Others believe that the Foreign Office encouraged the negative decision on CERN by suggesting that other European governments would follow a British lead. Again, although the British government is determined to find some agreement with the German and Dutch governments on the development of gas centrifuges for the enrichment of uranium, basic information on the decision has not been forthcoming.

This reticence on the part of the government is particularly regrettable since there is still an urgent need for more discussion to overcome the mystery of government decision-making; it is especially unwise at a time when the government is complaining that it is misunderstood by the British press. In Washington, for instance, the right of the public to join in debates on policy is much more securely part of the tradition of democratic discussion than it is in this country. Particularly disappointing is HM Government's support of the Fulton Committee's recommendation that discussion at the formative stage of policy-making between civil servants and ministers should remain confidential. The government say that only in this way can there be mutual trust between colleagues and proper critical discussion of different hypotheses. Yet the only basis for withholding information from the public should be that it affects national security or some other major public interest, and in this case it would seem that people are protecting their own rather than the national interests.

Conclusion

During the pre-election auction phase of early 1970 the political parties began to offer new deals to industry, to create, so the argument went, greater efficiency. The Conservative package included a disengagement in government relations with industry, and a close fight with the unions. Neither course was really relevant to the problems facing either industry or the country as a whole, and the combination offered a prospect of disaster.

The Labour Party's contribution was the mid-1969 statement, "Labour's Economic Strategy", whose proposals seemed to suggest that Labour takes a long time to learn from the errors of its previous industrial policies. The problems of the real industrial world were hardly touched on, except for two proposals which aimed to meet an essential gap in governmental policy in recent years. These were: a national investment board to co-ordinate existing industrial bodies, and a State Holding Company to promote new public enterprise. The reference to the employees' charter was not new and nothing was added to suggest how it might be achieved. The 1970 Industrial Relations Bill introduced just before the Election did go a little further but it still showed a lack of courage in tackling the problem of industrial democracy.

It seems, then, the greatest improvement in government-industrial relations will only take place when government, as the main communicator, begins to anticipate future developments and does not simply react to pressures when events force it to do so.

APPENDIX I

For the purposes of this study it is of interest to note only the responsibilities of departments and establishments which are related to industry:

The Cabinet Office	acts as a "Private Secretary" to the Cabinet, responsibility for National Economic Development Council.
Treasury	responsible for economic policy; internally for developing management services, including organization and methods work, enquiries into comparisons of management practices.
Ministry of Agriculture, Fisheries and Food	administers deficiency payment schemes and various grants and subsidies designed to improve the efficiency of the industries; gives free technical advice; determines the role of agriculture and forestry in the economy.
Board of Customs and Excise	collects and administers customs and excise duties.
Ministry of Defence	includes research, development and production, sales and procurement of equipment.

Department of Education and Science — a key function relates to the appraisal and training of manpower; conducts research through the following research councils: Medical, Agricultural, Natural Environment, Social Science, and Science; educational functions include training teachers, building schools, etc.

Foreign and Commonwealth Office — provides communication between British and foreign governments on all matters supporting trade.

Home Office — control of employment of children and young persons.

Department of Local Government and Regional Planning — co-ordination of work of Ministries of Housing and Local Government and Transport; local government reform; concerned with housing, development of land, Land Commission, National Park Commission, Water Resources Board, Commission for New Towns.

Central Office of Information — information services to industry.

Board of Inland Revenue — administers laws relating to income tax and surtax, capital gains tax, Corporation tax, stamp duty, estate duty, etc.

Department of Employment and Productivity — concerned with prices and incomes, distribution of manpower between industries and occupations, administers the Industrial Training Act, supervises industry through the Factory Inspectorate; promotes good industrial relations; provides for conciliation, arbitration

	and investigation of industrial disputes, administers Redundancy Payment Act of 1965, Wages Councils Act 1959, Selective Employment Payments Act 1966, employment exchanges; productivity services to industry.
Ministry of Overseas Development	includes management of capital and technical assistance overseas, responsible for a number of research organizations.
Post Office	may be considered as a nationalized industry for our purposes; carries on scientific research.
Ministry of Public Building and Works	point of contact within the government for the construction industries; responsible for Building Research Station.
Department of Health and Social Security	administers amongst others, National Health and Welfare Services, National Insurance (Industrial Injuries) Acts; Supplementary Benefits Commission; does certain refunds of the selective employment tax.
Government Social Survey Department	research body dealing with social and economic problems, provides statistics and facts to all other departments on request.
Ministry of Transport	responsible for nationalized transport industries (British Railways Board, London Transport Board, British Transport Docks Board, British Waterways Board, Transport Holding Company).

MINISTRY OF TECHNOLOGY

Responsibility for the government's relationship with the engineering and vehicles industries: This is a responsibility partly for handling the problems which these industries present to the government, and partly for initiating action to foster their economic and technological development.

Merchant shipbuilding: The main task here is to carry out through the Shipbuilding Industry Board the reconstruction of the industry proposed in the Geddes Report.

The United Kingdom Atomic Energy Authority: Responsibility for the monies provided to the Authority by Parliament, and for major policy directions; deployment of the Authority's important research and development resources, and with the restructuring of the nuclear plant industry.

Government research establishments: Control of sixteen research establishments, with a total staff of some 22,000. Including UKAEA establishments, the total manpower engaged in research and development is about 6,000 qualified (graduate equivalent) engineers and scientists. In addition, the Ministry supports forty-three industrial research associations with about 1,800 qualified men. The Minister is responsible for the National Research Development Corporation which is currently handling over three hundred development projects with an investment of over £25 million.

Responsibility for the government's relationship with the aircraft and aerospace industries: This involves the development and support of civil aircraft, ranging from the supersonic Concorde to Beagle light aircraft; the follow-up to the Plowden Report; and space technology and policy, both nationally and in international institutions.

Government procurement of aircraft, electronics and other equipment for defence purposes: This is the biggest procurement task in government—over £400 million a year—and by far the biggest operation of the Ministry, in terms of staff and money engaged. It involves a close link with the Ministry of Defence.

A general responsibility for fostering technological advance: This embraces a wide range of tasks undertaken in support of industry: the operation of productivity and advisory services; the extension of standards, nationally and internationally, and financial support for the British Standards Institution; quality assurance schemes; the metrication programme; the dissemination of technical information; and (with the professional institutions) work to strengthen the engineering profession, to improve quantity and quality in the supply of engineers, and to help the development of engineering generally.

Fuel and Power: Since the merger with the Ministry of Power, responsibility for all primary fuels and plant industries for electricity generation, together with other power and energy supply and plant industries.

Industrial Reorganization Corporation: Responsibility for IRC arises from concern with the structure of industry and industrial productivity.

Mineral Development: The industries concerned with mineral development in both the public and private sectors, except those which are closely linked with the construction industry.

Distribution of Industry: General distribution of industry, regional economic development and industrial liaison advisory services.

Investment Grants: Administration of the system of investment grants for industry.

BOARD OF TRADE

General responsibility for the nation's commerce and overseas trade, responsible for commercial relations with foreign countries, tariffs, dumping, exports, trade fairs, companies, consumer protection, statistics of trade and industry, shipping, and civil aviation.

Within the divisions of the Board, the following services are provided.

Trade divisions: Commercial Relations and Exports: Responsibility for general external commercial policy including General

Agreement on Tariffs and Trade (GATT), the United Nations Conference on Trade and Development (UNCTAD), the Organization for Economic Cooperation and Development (OECD), the Council of Europe, the European Coal and Steel Community (ECSC), the European Free Trade Association (EFTA) and the European Economic Community (EEC). The Divisions are assisted overseas by Commercial Officers of the Diplomatic Service.

Export Policy and Promotion Division: These services include British Weeks, Licensing, Export Rebate Certificates.

Economic Divisions: Matters concerned with consumer protection, including the administration of the Merchandise Marks Acts; weights and measures legislation; credit trading, including hire purchase and hiring. The advertising industry. Tourism and the holiday and hotel trades. Monopolies, mergers and restrictive practices, including resale price maintenance.

Tariff Divisions: Responsibility for policy in respect of the United Kingdom protective tariff and for international tariff negotiations. Consideration of applications for changes in import duties, for suspension of duties, for the imposition of anti-dumping and countervailing duties, for drawback and for remission of duty.

Shipping Policy Division: Policy on UK Merchant fleet.

Marine Division: Administration of marine legislation.

Civil Aviation Divisions: All aspects of commercial and economic policy affecting civil aviation, including air service licensing legislation, policy planning and management of State-owned civil aerodromes, aircraft noise, standards.

Statistics Division: The collection and/or analysis of various statistics, including those relating to overseas trade, industrial production, shipping, conditions relating to the balance of payments.

Patent Office, Industrial Property and Copyright Department: Administration of the Acts on Industrial Property and Copyright.

Insurance and Companies Department and Bankruptcy Department: Administration of the Companies Acts, the Registration of Business Names Act, the Prevention of Fraud (Investments) Act which regulates the business of dealing in securities and Unit trusts.

In addition, there are a number of services divisions dealing with accounts and information.

APPENDIX II

Investment Grants

Investment grants are available on capital expenditure for the manufacturing, construction and extractive industries to cover new plant and machinery.

The national rate of grant is 20 per cent of the capital cost of such plant and machinery but a 40 per cent rate is payable on assets for use in development areas.

Computers, ships and hovercraft acquired by persons carrying on a business in Britain are also eligible for grants. The rate in these cases is 20 per cent (25 per cent in 1967 and 1968), except that computers for industrial use in the development areas may in certain circumstances be eligible for grants at the development area rate.

Assistance for projects providing employment in development areas Buildings

Premises are provided for rent or purchase. Companies renting a government factory for a new project may qualify for an initial rent-free period of two years where, in the government's opinion, special problems have been involved in setting up new projects at a considerable distance from the company's undertaking. In the special development areas new projects may qualify for a rent-free period of up to 5 years in a government factory.

Building Grants

Building grants are normally available to cover up to 25 per cent of building costs. If a company is setting up a new project a long way from its existing undertaking, 35 per cent may be given. In the special development areas new projects may qualify for 35 per cent building grants and loans, at moderate rates of interest, towards the balance of building costs.

Loans and Grants for General Expenditure

Loans for buying or building premises are available in special development areas even where the Ministry of Technology is providing the premises or a building grant. Loans can be made for plant, machinery and equipment (excluding the amount of any investment grant) and for working capital.

In the special development areas new projects may qualify for operational grants for three years, normally at the rate of 10 per cent a year, based on the cumulative expenditure on eligible buildings, plant and machinery (less any building or investment grant).

Consultancy Grants

A nine-month pilot scheme has operated in the Bristol and Glasgow areas under which grants of 50 per cent of approved expenditure were made available to small companies for the employment of consultants and other expert business advisers.

Exports

There are a number of schemes for helping with overseas trade promotions, trade missions, market research, as well as providing trade directories.

Grants and Allowances to Workers Accepting Work Away from Home

The Department of Employment and Productivity operates three schemes which, by helping workers to take up employment away from home, also assist employers to recruit workers from other areas.

Resettlement Transfer Scheme

To assist unemployed workers, with poor employment prospects in their home areas, to move to other areas to take jobs

which cannot be filled by local labour. Assistance is available
for up to two years from the date of transfer and includes free
and assisted fares, settling-in grants of £5 a week, lodging allowances of 70s. and, where household removal is involved, a
contribution towards the legal and other costs of selling and
buying a house within a limit of £120.

Key Workers Scheme

This scheme assists employed workers to transfer to key posts
in work which their employers are setting up or extending in
development areas.

Nucleus Labour Force Scheme

This scheme assists companies who are setting up factories in
areas of high unemployment. Certain of the facilities of the
resettlement transfer scheme are available to unemployed
workers who are recruited in the new area, and given training,
prior to their return to form a nucleus of trained labour in the
new factory.

Industrial Training Schemes

Details of grants towards the current and capital expenses
incurred in training can be obtained from Industrial Training
Boards, and of grants to assist training of "green" labour in
development areas from any employment exchange.

BIBLIOGRAPHY

GOVERNMENT

Bailey, S. D., *English Parliamentary Democracy* (2nd ed.), Boston, 1962.

—— (ed.), *The British Party System—A Symposium* (2nd ed.), London, 1953.

Bane, W. T., *Operational research, models and government*, No. 8, C.A.S., HMSO Occasional Paper, Nov. 1968.

Benemy, F. W. G., *The Elected Monarch, The Development of the Powers of the Prime Minister*, London, 1965.

Burns, Sir Alan (ed.), *Parliament as an Export*, London, 1966.

Carter, B. E., *The Office of the Prime Minister*, London, 1956.

Coombes, D., *The Member of Parliament and the Administration—The Case of the Select Committee on Nationalized Industries*, Allen and Unwin, London, 1966.

Emden, C. S., *The People and the Constitution. Being a History of the Development of the People's Influence in British Government* (2nd ed.), Oxford, 1956.

Felstein, M. S., "Cost-Benefit Analysis and Investment in the Public Sector", *Public Administration*, XCII, Winter, 1964.

Gordon Walker. P., *The Cabinet*, Cape, 1970.

Hanson, A. H., *Parliament and Public Ownership*, Cassell, London, 1961.

Jennings, Sir Ivor, *Parliament* (2nd ed.), Cambridge, 1957.

—— *Cabinet Government* (3rd ed.), Cambridge, 1959.

—— *The British Constitution* (4th ed.), Cambridge, 1961.

Laski, H. J., *Parliamentary Government in England*, London, 1938.

Mackintosh, J. P., *The British Cabinet*, London, 1962.

Morrison, H., *Government and Parliament—A Survey from the Inside* (3rd ed.), London, 1964.

Robertson, J. H., *The design of information-processing systems for government,* No. 1, C.A.S. Occasional Paper, HMSO, April 1967.

Wade, E. C. S., and Phillips, G. G., *Constitutional Law* (7th ed.), London, 1965.

Williams, Alan, *Output budgetting and the contribution of micro-economics to efficiency in government,* No. 4, C.A.S. Occasional Paper, HMSO, April 1967.

INDUSTRY

Action Society Trust, *Studies in Nationalized Industry* (series edited by G. R. Taylor) Claygate and London, 1950–3.

No. 1 : *Accountability to Parliament*
No. 2 : *The Powers of the Minister*
No. 3 : *Problems of Promotion Policy*
No. 4 : *The Men on the Boards*
No. 5 : *The Miners' Pension*
No. 6 : *The Extent of Centralization, I*
No. 7 : *The Extent of Centralization, II*
No. 8 : *The Future of the Unions*
No. 9 : *Patterns of Organization*
No. 10 : *The Framework of Joint Consultation*
No. 11 : *The Workers' Point of View*
No. 12 : *Relations with the Public*

Allen, G. C., *British Industries and their Organization* (4th ed.), Longmans, London, 1959.

Bendix, *Work and Authority in Industry,* John Wiley and Sons, Inc., New York, 1956.

Burn, D. (ed.), *The Structure of British Industry,* Vols. 1 and 2, National Institute of Economic and Social Research, London, 1959.

Carter, C. F., and Williams, B. R., *Industry and Technical Progress,* Oxford University Press, London, 1957.

—— *Investment in Innovation,* Oxford University Press, London, 1958.

Clegg, H. A., *Industrial Democracy and Nationalization,* Blackwell, Oxford, 1951.

Cox, D. and Dyce Sharp, K. M., "Research on the Unit of Work", *Occup. Psychol.*, 25, 90, 1951.

Evely, R. and Little, I. M. D., *Concentration in British Industry,* Cambridge University Press, 1960.

Florence, P. Sargent, *The Logic of British and American Industry,* Routledge and Kegan Paul, 1953.

—— *Industry and the State,* Hutchinson University Library, 1957.

—— *Post-war Investment, Location and Size of Plant,* National Institute of Economic and Social Research, Occasional Papers 29, C.U.P., Cambridge, 1962.

Goodman, E., *Forms of Public Control and Ownership,* Christophers, London, 1951.

Guenault, P. H., and Jackson, J. H., *The Control of Monopoly in the United Kingdom,* Longmans, London, 1960.

Hart, P. E., "Business Concentration in the United Kingdom", *Journal of the Royal Statistical Society,* 123, Part 2 (1960), pp. 50–58.

Jewkes, J. and others, *The Sources of Invention,* Macmillan, London, 1958.

Kelf-Cohen, R. *Nationalization in Britain: The End of a Dogma* (2nd ed.), Macmillan, London, 1961.

Moonman, E., *The Manager and the Organization,* Tavistock, London, 1961.

—— *Communication in an Expanding Organization,* Tavistock, London, 1970.

N.I.I.P., *The Training of Workers within the Factory,* OEEC, Paris, 1957.

Shanks, Michael, *The Innovators,* Pelican Original, 1967.

Sheahan, John, *Promotion and Control of Industry in Postwar France,* Harvard University Press, Cambridge Mass, 1963.

OF GENERAL INTEREST

Allen, G. C., "The British Economy", *Economic Systems of the West,* (ed.), Rudolf Frei, Tubingen, J. C. B. Mohr (Paul Siebeck), 1, 1957, pp. 65–99.

—— *Japan's Economic Recovery*, London and New York, Oxford University Press, 1960.

Ajia Kyokai, *An Outline of Japanese Industry*, Asia Kyokai, Tokyo, 1955.

Ashton, T. S., *The Industrial Revolution, 1760–1830*, Oxford University Press, London, 1948.

Baum, W., *The French Economy and the State*, Rand Corporation Research Study, Princeton University Press, Princeton, 1958.

Buxbaum, R., "Anti-Trust Regulation within the European Economic Community", *Columbia Law Review*, 61 (1961), pp. 402–409.

Calcatierra, E., Mazzocchi, G., Lombardini, S., and Vito, F., "The Main Outlines of the Structure of the Italian Economy", in *Economic Systems of the West*, (ed.), R. Frei, Tubingen, J. C. B. Mohr (Paul Siebeck), 2, 1957, p. 81.

Capronnier, Francois, *La Crise de l'industrie cotonniere, francaise*, Editions Genin, Paris, 1959.

Economic News from Italy, *Italy's 200 Largest Companies*, Elite Publishing Company, New York, March, 1962.

Enterprise, *Les 500 Premières Sociétés francaises*, No. 316, Paris, 23 September, 1961.

Goetz-Girey, R., *Monopoly and Competition in France*, in Monopoly and Competition and their Regulation, ed. Edward Chamberlin, Macmillan, London, 1954, pp. 21–42.

Hackett, J. and Hackett, Anne-Marie, *Economic Planning in France*, Allen and Unwin, London, 1963.

Hammond, J. L., and Hammond, Barbara, *The Town Labourer, 1760–1832*.

Hegeland, H., "The Structure and Functioning of Sweden's Political Economy," in *Economic Systems in the West*, (ed.), R. Frei, Tubingen, J. C. B. Mohr (Paul Siebeck), 1, 1957, pp. 213–242.

Lewis, W. Arthur, *The Theory of Economic Growth*, Allen and Unwin, London, 1955.

Lutz, Vera, *Italy, A Study in Economic Development*, Royal

Institute of International Affairs, Oxford University Press, London, 1962.

Nelson, R. L., *Concentration in the Manufacturing Industries of the United States*, Yale University Press, New Haven, 1963.

Oppenheimer, J. R., *The Open Mind*, New York, Simon and Schuster, 1955.

P.E.P., *Government and Industry*, P.E.P., London, 1952.

P.E.P., *Growth in the British Economy*, Allen and Unwin, London, 1960.

Ricardo, D., *The Principles of Political Economy and Taxation*, Cambridge, C.U.P., Cambridge, 1951.

Robinson E. A. G., (ed.), *Economic Consequences of the Size of Nations* (proceedings at conference held by International Economic Association), St. Martin's Press, New York, 1960.

Sampson, A., *Anatomy of Britain* (2nd ed.), London, 1965.

Scitovsky, T., *Economic Theory and Western European Integration*, Allen and Unwin, London, 1958.

Veblen, T., *The Theory of Business Enterprise*, Charles Scribner's Sons, New York, 1919.

INDEX